LILLIAN
JEN

2011
fortune & feng shui
DOG

Congratulations!

I want to thank and congratulate you for investing in yourself...and in the latest edition of Fortune and Feng Shui...your personalized horoscope book for 2011!

What will you be earning one year from today? How will you look and feel one year from today...and will you be happier?

In this little book Jennifer and I reveal many insights pertaining to your particular animal sign...what you can expect and how to protect and enhance all areas of your life for success in 2011.

And why stop here?

I'd like to also extend a personal invitation to you to join my Mandala...and receive my FREE online weekly newsletter...Lillian Too's Mandala Ezine.

You'll discover other powerful feng shui secrets from me that go hand-in-hand with the valuable information in this book. And it's absolutely FREE... delivered to your in box weekly!

Lillian Too's Online Weekly Ezine... FREE!

You've taken the first step to success by purchasing this book. Now expand your horizons and learn more about authentic feng shui that really works...including more about the powerful 3rd dimension...your inner feng shui!
Just go to www.lilliantoomandalaezine.com and register today!

It's EASY! It's FREE! It's FRESH and it's delivered to you WEEKLY

Don't miss out! It's easy to register at www.lilliantoomanadalaezine.com and you'll also receive a special BONUS from me when you register today! I look forward to visiting with you online!

All the best!
Lillian

Lillian's online FREE weekly ezine is only available when you register online at *www.lillantoomandalaezine.com*

Fortune & Feng Shui 2011 DOG
by Lillian Too and Jennifer Too
© 2011 Konsep Lagenda Sdn Bhd

Text © 2011 Lillian Too and Jennifer Too
Photographs and illustrations © WOFS.com Sdn Bhd

The moral right of the authors to be identified as authors of this book has been asserted.

Published by KONSEP LAGENDA SDN BHD (223 855)
Kuala Lumpur 59100 Malaysia

For more Konsep books, go to www.lillian-too.com or www.wofs.com
To report errors, please send a note to errors@konsepbooks.com
For general feedback, email feedback@konsepbooks.com

Notice of Rights
All rights reserved. No part of this publication may be reproduced, stored in a retrieval system or transmitted in any form, or by any means, electronic, mechanical, photocopying, recording, or otherwise, without the prior written permission of the publisher. For information on getting permission for reprints and excerpts, contact: permissions@konsepbooks.com

Notice of Liability
The information in this book is distributed on an "As Is" basis, without warranty. While every precaution has been taken in the preparation of the book, neither the author nor Konsep Lagenda shall have any liability to any person or entity with respect to any loss or damage caused or alleged to be caused directly or indirectly by the instructions contained in this book.

ISBN 978-967-329-041-3
Published in Malaysia, August 2010

DOG BORN CHART

BIRTH YEAR	WESTERN CALENDAR DATES	AGE	KUA NUMBER MALES	KUA NUMBER FEMALES
Wood Dog	14 Feb 1934 to 3 Feb 1935	77	3 East Group	3 East Group
Fire Dog	2 Feb 1946 to 21 Jan 1947	65	9 East Group	6 West Group
Earth Dog	18 Feb 1958 to 7 Feb 1959	53	6 West Group	9 East Group
Metal Dog	6 Feb 1970 to 26 Jan 1971	41	3 East Group	3 East Group
Water Dog	25 Jan 1982 to 12 Feb 1983	29	9 East Group	6 West Group
Wood Dog	10 Feb 1994 to 30 Jan 1995	17	6 West Group	9 East Group
Fire Dog	29 Jan 2006 to 17 Feb 2007	5	3 East Group	3 East Group

CONTENTS

RABBIT YEAR 2011 - GENERAL OUTLOOK
Drastically Clashing Elements With
Potential For Wealth   9

2. DOG ENJOYS
A YEAR OF VAST POTENTIAL
Staying On Top Of Your Horoscope Luck   42
- Fire Dog – 65 years – Setbacks but finances stay strong   56
- Earth Dog – 53 years – Confidence required to succeed   57
- Metal Dog – 41 years – Feeling energized & moving ahead   58
- Water Dog – 29 years – Auspicious financials empower you   59
- Wood Dog – 17 years – Good health; peaceful year   60

3. DISCOVERING YOUR LUNAR MANSIONS
The Influence Of Your Sky Animal Sign   61

4. INTERACTING WITH OTHERS IN 2010
Dog's Excellent Feng Shui Winds Hides Its Vulnerability 84

- Dog With Rat – Conflicts through the year 98
- Dog With Ox – Ups and downs through a jolly year 100
- Dog With Tiger – Amazing pair and very auspicious too 102
- Dog With Rabbit – Shoulder for Rabbit to lean on 104
- Dog With Dragon – Natural enemies find common ground 106
- Dog With Snake – Attraction is mutual and full of sparks 108
- Dog With Horse – Allies bite off more than they can chew 110
- Dog With Sheep – Can find companionship and love 112
- Dog With Monkey – Cosmic sparks fly between this pair 114
- Dog With Rooster – A hollow feeling generates distance 116
- Dog With Dog – Bringing out best & worst in one another 118
- Dog With Boar – Easy going relationship 120

5. MONTHLY ANALYSES OF YOUR LUCK
Good Timing of Month Stars Helps Dog 122

February 2011 – Starting the year right 123
March 2011 – Good fortune doubles 126
April 2011 – Feeling of being double-crossed 129
May 2011 – Great month with powerful top level support 132
June 2011 – Minor setbacks affect your confidence 135
July 2011 – Romantic attraction engages your emotions 138
August 2011 – Hostility leads to intolerance 141
September 2011 – Health ailments can get serious 144
October 2011 – Emerging victorious over bad vibes 147
November 2011 – New blue oceans for your business 150

December 2011 – Ending the year on a very high note 153
January 2012 – Getting rid of the bad apples in your basket 156

6. IMPORTANT FENG SHUI UPDATES FOR 2011
159
- Suppressing flying star afflictions of the year 168
- Dealing with Right and Left of Dog's luck 192
- Activating the trinity of Tien Ti Ren luck 196
- Magnifying Earth element to enhance resources 209
- Nine Wealth Gods to materialize prosperity luck 214

7. POWERFUL TALISMANS & AMULETS FOR 2011
216
- Protective Pendants - to suppress Three Killings energy 217
- 3 Celestial Protectors - dispel Three Killings Chi 218
- Sacred Sunburst - counter low Life Force & Inner Essence 219
- Enhancing Mirror - to absorb power of 8 from Northwest 219
- Flaming Dharma Wheel - suppress misunderstanding 220
- Sacred Mantra Plaque - against Cosmic Negatives 221
- Water Globe with Tree of Life - enhance home direction 221
- Earth Chi Enhancing Stones 222
- Sacred Moving Mantra Watches 222
- Table Top Treasures 224
- Powerful Gemstones 226

RABBIT YEAR 2011
Clashing Elements
But Economically Better

The year of the Golden Rabbit 2011 will be a noisy year filled with the sounds of clashing elements. Global energy continues to be discordant. But it is a year when most of the animal signs enjoy the potential to make genuinely good advances economically. There is money to be made.

In fact, for those who are able to tap into their veins of good fortune, 2011 can turn out to be a bonanza year. It is a year that favors animal signs located in the secondary compass directions and is less favorable to those occupying cardinal directions. So two thirds of the animal signs can look forward to improving their financial situation.

We examine three important indicators to determine the year's outlook when the diplomatic, soft-hearted Rabbit rules, taking center stage and bringing a new set of energies to the fortunes of the world. After the dramatic earthquakes, landslides and volcanic eruptions of the Tiger Year, can we welcome in a quieter, safer and more stable year? Alas, if the charts are any indication, it seems not; there are deep rumblings under the earth; natural disasters and discordant chi continues to pose a threat to our safety; these calamities threaten different parts of the world. Earth's environment needs time to settle but for most individuals, happily the outlook does not look that dire. There is more good luck than bad for most of the animal signs.

Outlook for the 12 Animals

In 2011, those of you born in the year of the **Dog** can smile as you will be going through a year of excellent potential. The Dog is helped by the year's Rabbit energy, being the Rabbit's secret friend. It also benefits from great feng shui winds brought by the incomparable energy of 8! Sure, you will be affected by the year's discordant energies, but you are strong enough; and it does not require much effort on your part to overcome the year's conflicts.

With the powerful Northwest as your home location, all the attributes of the patriarchal Chien trigram will get activated by the supremacy of 8, so you will possess the muscle to walk vigorously through the year. Make sure to imbue your work with great intensity of purpose. Use the luck clout that has flown into your direction with focus and concentration and push all distractions aside. No matter what your goal may be, you have the capacity to fulfill them. So stay confident and strong, and flow with the good energy of the year. Let the good winds carry you to new highs and enjoy the ride.

The **Boar** enjoys the same kind of luck energy as the Dog, being also influenced by the powerful 8 and benefiting from the Chien trigram attributes getting activated, but Boar needs to watch that success luck does not diminish. Boar needs to stay updated and check to make sure neither their main door nor their bedrooms are afflicted this year.

In 2011, the cardinal East and West animal rulers, **Rabbit** and **Rooster** are afflicted by harmful energy and need to stay alert. These two must watch their backs, as both signs are affected. East and West are strongly afflicted directions.

The Rabbit in 2011 is hit by the nasty *wu wang* or five yellow, which is a powerful and nasty feng shui affliction. This is a negative star number that brings ill winds of misfortune and it must be subdued. The Rabbit (Dog's secret friend) must protect itself against the *wu wang* star affliction. The remedy for the *wu wang* must be strong enough to overcome its power. Thus for 2011, we are bringing out a remedy - the five element pagoda - that also has the tree of life which symbolizes the supremacy of the Rabbit's Wood element over the Earth element of the five yellow. This is the most important thing for the Rabbit to put in place - the cure for the *wu wang*!

The **Rooster** meanwhile sits on the *Disaster Energy Star* in the West and must contend with the *Three Killings* affliction. These are bad winds which must be subdued before Rooster can benefit from favorable feng shui brought by the number 9 star.

The **Snake** continues to have a good year in 2011 as it benefits from excellent feng shui winds. This is a year when continuous good fortune comes and brings big as well as small success. The Snake enjoys excellent indications of good fortune brought by the 24 mountain stars and will definitely be on a big roller coaster ride in 2011.

The **Ox** enjoys a wonderful year as it benefits from the double *Big Auspicious* stars that flank its astrological location. This together with its number 1 star ensures that good fortune manifests strongly. Meanwhile, inviting a Deity figure into the home brings good luck as the Ox has the *Golden Deity Star* in its chart this year.

The **Rat** and the **Horse (Dog's ally)** also enjoy the promise of good fortune, but whether or not they can actually cause this good luck potential to materialize will depend on their own inventiveness. But doing well in 2011 does not come without a share of the year's discordance. **Horse** has a tendency to get sick, while **Rat's** normally calm demeanor is put out of sorts by quarrelsome impulses brought by the hostility star.

The **Dragon** should sail through 2011 with a series of small successes. For the Dragon, heaven luck shines bright, so there could be unexpected windfalls. The way to go is for the Dragon to enhance for special luck to manifest. Wearing and displaying good luck charms will be beneficial.

The **Sheep** benefits from the year, but only when there is an adequate supply of Earth element energy, so this sign needs strengthening with the **Earth Seal**. It also benefits to display and wear raw crystal and natural quartz crystal. Large reconstituted crystal globes are of benefit.

The **Monkey** will have a harder time staying ahead of the competition, especially those working professionally pursuing a career. Those doing business need to be careful not to get conned. This sign could fall victim to external politicking. The Monkey must be wary and alert to false friends and ambitious colleagues. It is beneficial to carry amulets that fight against the evil eye!

Finally, the **Tiger** (Dog's ally) has to work at generating heaven luck energy by wearing the **Heaven Seal**. Doing so brings good fortune. This is a year when depending on its own instincts is more beneficial than listening to others.

The Year's Four Pillars

The first indicator we look at to get an overall feel for the destiny outlook for the year is the year's Four Pillars chart. This offers a snapshot of the year and reveals the hidden forces that affect the fortunes of the year. To know what's in store, we analyze the eight elements that dominate the four pillars i.e. the heavenly stems and earthly branches that rule the chi energies of the year.

The preceding Tiger Year was a year of unstable earth disasters characterized by rogue waves in the seas and big earthquakes that began at the start of the year and continued unabated through the year... from Chile to

Japan to Turkey to Indonesia to China and Taiwan. Last year, hidden Earth energies rumbled and brought tragedy to many parts of the globe.

In this coming year 2011 of the Golden Metallic Rabbit, its Four Pillars Chart looks rather foreboding. In fact, the chart is indicating not one pillar of directly clashing elements, but FOUR!

PAHT CHEE CHART 2011 - GOLDEN RABBIT			
HOUR	DAY	MONTH	YEAR
HEAVENLY STEM	HEAVENLY STEM	HEAVENLY STEM	HEAVENLY STEM
壬	庚	庚	辛
YANG WATER	YANG METAL	YANG METAL	YIN METAL
EARTHLY BRANCH	EARTHLY BRANCH	EARTHLY BRANCH	EARTHLY BRANCH
丙午	甲寅	甲寅	乙卯
FIRE HORSE	WOOD TIGER	WOOD TIGER	WOOD RABBIT
HIDDEN HEAVENLY STEMS OF THE YEAR			
YANG FIRE YANG EARTH	YANG FIRE YANG EARTH YANG WOOD	YANG FIRE YANG EARTH YANG WOOD	YIN WOOD

The year is desperately short of EARTH ie Resource

Yes, all four of the pillars have discordant crushing energies, with three pillars indicating Metal crushing Wood, instantly telling us that the Rabbit of 2011 is not going to be a docile one. The remaining pillar has **Water destroying Fire**. So in 2011, all four pillars that make up the Eight Characters chart of the year are showing direct clashes. This is a nasty indication and it is a clear warning for everyone to be careful and circumspect.

Travel and risk-taking are best kept to a minimum, and it is a good idea to be prepared at all times. It is not a year to tempt fate. This is a general but potent piece of advice for the year. Better to stay home than to travel. Better to stay safe than to take risks. Just glance quickly at the chart and instantly you will see that in the DAY, MONTH and YEAR pillars, Metal is destroying Wood! These are direct clashes and here we see both yin and yang pillars having the same clashing characteristics.

And then in the HOUR pillar, Water is destroying Fire! Each one of the four pillars indicates extremely negative outlooks for the year; so from year start to year end, and affecting all age groups, hostile energies dominate. This has to be a record of some kind; to have all four pillars showing a clash of elements with the heavenly stem elements destroying the earthly branches in every single pillar of the chart.

Disharmony is thus the prominent force of the coming year and despite the Rabbit, usually an icon of diplomacy, it appears that feng shui cosmic forces this year bring plenty of high octane anger and intolerance. In addition, the chart also show the presence of two Tigers, which suggests that the Tiger energies of 2010 have not entirely abated. We face a scenario not unlike that of the previous year, but maybe worse; clashing elements are always indicators of hard times, so the energy of the year looks discordant.

The chart shows Metal and Wood dominating, with Metal energy having the upper hand. The essence of the year is Metal, but it is neither weak nor strong Metal. Although we see three Metal, the Water and Fire of the HOUR pillar destroys and weakens the Metal. And because there is no Earth element present in the chart, Metal lacks the resources to stay strong.

There appears to be a lack of resources during the year, and this is another bad sign. The absence of Earth also suggests an unbalanced chart, which is an indication of turmoil.

With this obvious imbalance, the prevailing attitude during the year is one of unrelenting intolerance. There are three Metals indicating the presence of competitive pressures, but the strength of the Metals cannot be sustained because of the lack of Earth. This indicates that competitive pressures cannot be sustained and it is best to not be pushed into a corner by competitors. Try thinking outside the box instead of combating the competition!

The Good News

However, when we look at the hidden elements of the chart, the news for 2011 is not all bad. Underlying all the competing energy, lies the potential for the creation of much new wealth. There is hidden Earth bringing unexpected resources to fuel growth for the year, and there is also hidden Wood, indicating unexpected wealth.

Likewise, there is also hidden Fire, so the year does not lack for managerial capability. The exercise of authority and leadership plays a big role in transforming the cosmic forces in 2011. Results may not be evident in the year itself, but there is no denying the positive benefits of good leadership. As the NW patriarchal sector this year has the 8, the cosmic forces are aligned to help the patriarchs i.e. the leaders of the planet. So in the trinity of heaven, earth and man, *tien ti ren*, it will be Mankind energy that prevails and delivers success and results.

Herein lies the good news for those who are commercially minded and business motivated. 2011 is a year when plenty of prosperity-making opportunities are present. There are many direct as well as indirect wealth-making opportunities emerging.

Although what is apparently missing are direct resources as indicated by the element Earth, which is missing from the main chart, there are thankfully three hidden Earth element. This more than makes up for their absence in the main chart. In effect, the chart can now be said to be balanced with the presence of all five elements when the hidden elements are taken into account.

What is in very small supply however is the element of **Water**, which was completely missing last year.

In 2011, Water represents creativity, intelligence and common sense. Because it is in such short supply, everyone once again continues to benefit from the **Water** element. This is what will create Wood which stands for wealth this year. Water also exhausts Metal which is destroying the Wood element.

Thus the source of wealth creation in 2011 is Water; i.e. creativity - original and strategic thinking which will open the way to mining the year's prosperity. Much of this creativity will come from the younger generation.

This will be a year when those who have just joined the workforce, and those who have recently graduated out of school and college will be the source of new ideas. And because it is the year of the Rabbit, when the East sector comes into prominence, it is likely that those born as the eldest sons of their families will be the ones whose stars will shine brightly. This year benefits the eldest sons of families.

Rabbit Years have always been years of appeasement, when conflicts arising in preceding Tiger Years get resolved. Unfortunately, 2011 continues to be a year of global political upheavals.

For the Dog born however, life could not be rosier as Dog benefits from the supreme 8 which brings great good fortune.

The Golden Rabbit Year is challenging and full of intrigues. Unlike the direct confrontations of the previous year, this is a year when unexpected betrayals and underhand tactics become prevalent.

For the Dog, it is likely that you will negotiate your way through the year staying on top of power plays and political intrigues. Those of you feeling this darker side of the year's energy will need to have a positive and non-defeatist attitude; only then can the coming twelve months from February 4th 2011 to February 4th 2012 benefit you. Then in spite of discordant element indications, you can create and accumulate new assets.

There is wealth luck in 2011. The **Dog** can harness wealth luck very easily this year as the feng shui winds are bringing you benevolent luck. What is needed is a keen eye for opportunities. Think outside the box to create new markets for your service and your products. The global business scenario is changing fast. New technology and applications of this fast-developing new technology is racing ahead at breakneck speed.

Globally, there is more than one prominent player in the technology game. Increasingly, the world is feeling the presence of China. Note that Period 7 benefitted the

West, but it is the Northeast that is ruling the energies of the current Period 8. This Period favors China.

Both the year 2011 and the Period itself favors those who move fast and who have prepared themselves to penetrate uncharted territory, just like water. We borrow the term blue oceans to suggest the clever opening up of new areas for creating wealth. And it does not matter whether you live in the West or in the Northeast, if you can work with the cosmic forces of the year and the period, you are sure to benefit.

Water is Vital

This is once again a year when the Water element brings prosperity, although not in the same way it did in the previous year. Those of you who installed water features last year and benefited from them will benefit again from it.

Note that in 2011, we are seeing three Metal destroying three Wood - i.e. clashing directly. The **Metal** of the year's heavenly stems continuing to destroy the Tiger's intrinsic **Wood**. On the surface, this is not a good sign.

But Metal, when used with skill and under special circumstances, can transform Wood into something of greater value. So even as Metal destroys Wood, it can transform Wood into an object of value. What is great this year is that there is more than enough Wood to make up for whatever gets destroyed. Note from the Pillars chart there are 3 hidden Wood, so there is definitely wealth to be created and accumulated.

But clashing elements always suggest hostilities, so the wars of the world will not see any easing or closure. In 2011, fighting continues with little hope for reconciliation; competition in the commercial environment and between companies and countries get worse.

Mankind energy can be harnessed very effectively to overcome the discordant energies of heaven and earth this year. All the resources required are available, the only snag being they are hidden and so, not immediately obvious. But they are there!

Here we can use the third dimension of feng shui - the powerful inner chi dimension - to transform and enhance the space and time chi of 2011 at individual personalized levels. Irrespective of the discordance of Heaven and Earth, those of us who know how can still arrange our lives to benefit from the hidden forces of the year.

We can focus on the mankind chi within all of us - focus on strengthening it - and in so doing, more effectively harness the spiritual energy of the empowered self to overcome obstacles and emerge triumphant. There are methods and rituals we can use to subdue negative energies caused by the four sets of clashing elements.

We can also apply element therapy to bring about a much improved balance in the elements in our immediate environments; and there are symbolic cures, many made into amulets, that can subdue negative "*stars*".

The Commanding Star

A very positive aspect of the year 2011 is the appearance of the *Commanding Star,* an outstandingly auspicious star. Its appearance in the 2011 chart is brought about by the presence of the Earthly Branch of Horse in the Hour pillar and the Earthly branch of Tiger in the Day pillar. This excellent indication arises out of the ally relationship that exists between Horse and Tiger. Here, the *Commanding Star* suggests traits brought by these two fearless animal signs to the year. It brings good vibrations benefiting those who show courage and fortitude.

The *Commanding Star* suggests the presence of authority, power and influence luck for the year, benefiting those who find themselves in a leadership situation or those holding a position of authority.

Indeed, the year will benefit those who know how to use their positions of influence and power; so managers and leaders who have a clear idea of what their strategy or focus should be will benefit from this star, despite the clashing elements of the year. Leaders will find the energy of the year increases their charisma and their effectiveness. The exercise of authority will come easily.

> Those born in the years of the Dog are especially lucky as they are the major beneficiary of this side of the year's luck profile. The Dog's location is the Northwest which is host to the supreme 8 star. This is a year when the Dog can afford to take risks, stand for election or start something new.

What can be worrying about the Commanding Star is that both the elements of the Hour pillar - Water and Fire - are not good for the intrinsic element of the year. Here we see Fire destroying Metal, and Water exhausting Metal. Superficially then, it appears that the Commanding Star can turn ugly, bringing obstacles instead of opportunities.

For the Dog, there is less to worry about, as the Horse and Tiger are BOTH allies of the Dog. As such the Commanding Star will only benefit the Dog person. This is definitely going to be your year. Just make sure you do not do anything to spoil things for yourself.

Flying Stars of 2011

The feng shui chart of the year which lays out the location of the year's flying stars in 2011 is dominated by the energy of 7, a weak star; but being the reigning number, its effect cannot be overlooked. The number 7 is a Metal number that represents the negative side of relationships, symbolizing duplicity and treachery. The number adds fuel to the discordant vibes of the clashing elements of the Four Pillars. So even though the Rabbit Year is usually subdued, 2011 has a fair bit of confrontation. Global incidence of violence is likely to continue.

This is a year when intrigue and situational upheavals occur frequently; brought by a higher incidence of betrayals and unbridled ambitions. It is a year when the center of buildings, houses and offices benefit from Water energy to subdue the strength of 7.

SE SMALL AUSPICIOUS **6** SMALL AUSPICIOUS	**SOUTH** BIG AUSPICIOUS **2** BIG AUSPICIOUS	**SW** EARTH SEAL **4** ROBBERY STAR
EAST TAI SUI **5** 5 YELLOW	**7**	**WEST** 3 KILLINGS **9** 3 KILLINGS
HEAVEN SEAL **1** GOLDEN DEITY **NE**	BIG AUSPICIOUS **3** BIG AUSPICIOUS **NORTH**	YEARLY CONFLICT **8** YI DUO STAR **NW**

FLYING STAR CHART 2011 - GOLDEN RABBIT

Luckily, the number 7 is a weak star in the current Period of 8, so it is not difficult to subdue. Anything of a dark blue color is sufficient for keeping it under control. It is advisable to make the effort to suppress the number 7 in homes and offices. This brings protection for residents and prevents them from falling victim to external politicking and trouble-makers.

In 2011 it is beneficial to activate the power of Water in the home. Invest in a small water feature to create a small presence of moving water in the center grid of the home. Or you can place a **Rhino** or **Elephant** there. Together, these three remedies are excellent for suppressing the negative influence of 7.

The luck of the different sectors of any structure is influenced by the new energy brought by the year's feng shui chart, as this reveals the year's lucky and unlucky sectors for buildings, houses and apartments.

The chart for 2011 indicates different numbers in each of the nine grids in this 3 X 3 sector chart. This looks like the original Lo Shu square which plays such a big role in time dimension feng shui except that each year, the numbers placed in each grid change according to the center number. With 7 in the center, the other numbers are then placed around the grid sectors. This is what changes the pattern of energy in homes and offices from year to year.

The numbers play a big part in determining the "*luck outlook*" of animal signs arising from the fact that each of the twelve signs occupies a designated compass location. Thus the Dog person occupies the Northwest location which enjoys the 8 star number. As for the 24 mountain stars, the star affecting Dog's luck is the star of yearly conflict. In view of this, Dog must watch out for its personal safety. 2011 has plenty of conflict energy, so do tread carefully.

The stars of the 24 mountains are very influential. There are 108 different fortune stars but only a handful fly into the 24 mountain directions in any year. These bring auspicious or harmful influences, but they vary in strength and type each year.

Houses and animal signs are affected in similar measure by the 24 mountain stars. Some stars bring good luck, some bring misfortune, while others bring protection.

When your sign is negatively afflicted and your vitality gets weakened, you need to wear specific protective Taoist charms. These not only protect, they also increase the potential for making the best of good fortune luck brought by the star energies for your animal sign.

The **Annual Protection Amulet** is to used to overcome the afflictions year and enhance good fortune luck for the year 2011.

We have made different charms to match each animal sign's needs. What Dog needs are strong enhancing decorative objects, powerful syllables and word affirmations that strengthen its good luck. Dog people need to be reminded to stay positive and upbeat. Dog people also benefit carrying the talisman hanging that wards off the evil eye, as there will be envious glances being thrown your way. There are other talismans to attract good fortune as well. These are highlighted later in this book.

But your home must also be protected; only then can you attract good fortune, and no hindrances occur that cause you to miss out on opportunities that come your way. Study the section on the updates required and get the required cures for the afflicted sectors of your home using compass directions. This is what will safeguard your feng shui and ensure that you stay strong and healthy this year.

Not many people know that it is essential to be mentally and physically strong to attract good fortune. After making sure that all the annual afflictions in your home are suppressed you can attract good feng shui with powerful symbols of good fortune. But for these to be effective you must also stay healthy and strong. This is what brings you the yang vigor needed to actualize good fortune. This helps to generate the third dimension to your luck - which is the empowerment of the self. It is this that makes the difference between succumbing to bad luck or transforming it into good luck. The process of transformation requires powerful self empowering energy. More on this later.

Staying Updated Each Month

Meanwhile, note that the monthly updates are just as important as the annual ones. Monthly luck forecasts are the highlight of this book because good timing plays an important part in attracting good fortune; and avoiding misfortunes. To enjoy good luck through the year, you must update your month-to-month feng shui. So you must keep track of how cosmic energies affect your luck each month.

Every animal sign can be alerted to the high and low points of their year, and be warned against negative energy, as well as to spur you on during months when your chi energy is high.

When to lie low and when to be go bravely forth are important to maximizing the opportunities of the year, so irrespective of whether the year is good or bad, you can avoid pitfalls and missing out on opportunities that come your way.

Nothing beats being prepared against potential misfortune because this reduces their impact. Knowing the nature of misfortune - whether it is related to illness or accident, betrayal or plain bad luck - helps you cope when the misfortune does occur. What is better is that when you wear protective remedies, mantra amulets or talismans, these are very effective in warding off misfortune. Thus an important aspect of reading these books is to take note of the spikes and dips in your monthly luck focusing on Career, Business, Family, Love and Study luck.

The monthly readings analyze each month's Lo Shu numbers, element, trigram and paht chee luck pillars. These accurately identify your good and bad months; they generate valuable pointers on how to navigate safely and successfully through the year, effectively helping you get your timing right on important decisions and actions.

The recommendations in this book alert you to months when you are vulnerable to illness, accidents or dangers. We also highlight good luck months when exciting new opportunities are likely to come to you. Knowing *when* will give you a competitive edge on timing. You'll get better at coping with setbacks and overcoming obstacles that occur from month to month.

Improving Your Luck

Your luck can also be substantially improved through the placement of symbolic enhancers or remedies to the spaces you occupy. This is a book on the personalized approach for you to attract good luck. You will see as you delve deeper that there are many ways you can improve your personalized luck despite the year being afflicted for you.

> What you need to place in your compass sector changes from year to year. You must be sure of what exactly you need to place in your **Northwest location** in 2011, mainly to activate the star number 8 as well as to energize the **Chien trigram**. An excellent way to activate the corner is to place the number 8 in this corner - one made of crystal or metal would be excellent. It is also an excellent idea to place eight rod metal windchimes here.

Your luck is affected by the year's flying stars (shown in the feng shui chart) as well as the elements of the four pillars and the luck stars of the 24 mountains. How you react to the year's changing energies depend on the strength of your spirit essence and your life force. This year 2011 for all animal signs, both of these important indications stay the same as last year.

There is no change to your life force and spiritual strength, so all Dog sign people continue to experience the same energy as last year in these two areas. Only the success potential for everyone has changed. This section of the book has thus been shortened. In its place, we are introducing a new aspect that affect your fortunes.

The extra dimension we address this year is to introduce you to your Sky Animal sign. In addition to one's year of birth animal sign, destiny and attitudes are also influenced by one's Lunar Mansion. This is represented by one of the 28 Sky Animals that correspond to the 28 days in a typical month. This is your Day Sign and it interacts with your Year Sign to add important new dimensions to your compatibility with others, and to your luck outlook each year.

Your Lunar Mansion

This is based on the four great constellations that are the foundation of feng shui - the constellations of the *Green Dragon, Crimson Phoenix, Black Tortoise* and *White Tiger.*

The **Green Dragon** rules the Eastern skies, while the **Crimson Phoenix** rules the Southern skies. The **White Tiger** is Lord of the Western Skies and the **Black Tortoise** oversees the Northern skies. Collectively, they rule over the 28 Sky Animals, each having dominance over 7 of them. Depending on which of the 28 animals is your Day sign, you are under the influence of (and thus protected by) the Dragon, Tiger, the Phoenix or the Tortoise. These are termed the constellations of the Lunar Mansion.

Your Sky Animal brings additional insights to the kind of luck you enjoy in any given year depending on your profession or business. The year 2011 is ruled by the Eastern sign of the Rabbit; and with two Tigers in the Pillars chart, this is a year when the Green Dragon who rules the Eastern Skies is dominant. Those whose Day Sign comes under the mighty Dragon are more likely to benefit from the Dragon. The Dragon image was very beneficial last year and continues to be the celestial creature that brings good fortune to the year 2011. And since the Water element continues to be in short supply, it is as beneficial to have water and Dragon together, especially in the East of your home where it enhances the Rabbit Year, working with the Tiger presence in the Pillars chart to create the Zodiac trinity combination of Spring. But those born in a Dog year can skip inviting in the Dragon unless they are born under the Dragon constellation.

Determining your Lunar Mansion Day Animal requires access to specific calculations retrieved from the Chinese Almanac. In this book, these calculations have been simplified, and any one can quite easily work out their Day Animal sign from the chapter on your lunar mansion. These offer additional insights into your luck outlook for the year.

Updating Your Feng Shui

Buildings are affected by new energy patterns each year, so knowing how to work with these new energies is what unlocks good fortune each year. It is important to place remedial updates that safeguard the feng shui of your home and office. This aspect of feng shui is its time dimension, and because energy transforms at the start of the year, changing on the day of Spring (also referred to as the *lap chun*), it is beneficial for all updates to be done before this date, which falls on February 4th, 2011. This corresponds to the start of the solar year of the Chinese Hsia calendar.

Remedial cures are always necessary to subdue the effects of negative stars and malicious influences of bad luck numbers in the flying star chart. The location and strength of these negative influences change from year to year, so it is necessary to check them every year.

Three Dimensions in Feng Shui

Feng shui has three dimensions to its practice, a space, time and self-empowering dimension. These address the heaven, earth and mankind chi that make up the trinity of luck that collectively account for how luck works for or against us. If you want to benefit from total feng shui, you should use the collective power of all three dimensions.

Space dimension is governed by environmental feng shui methods - collectively practiced under the broad umbrella of what everyone terms feng shui. Here, it comprises the art of living in harmony with natural landforms and the art of placing auspicious objects with great symbolic meaning and element properties around us. Environmental feng shui takes note of compass directions on a personalized basis and use other methods that focus on lucky and unlucky sectors. Broadly speaking, it takes care of the Earth aspect in the trinity of luck.

Then there is *time dimension feng shui*, which requires our practice to take note of changing and transformational energies. These indicate that energy is never still; that it is constantly changing, and it is therefore necessary to always take cognizance of how energy transforms over various overlapping cycles of time; annually, monthly, daily, hourly and even in larger time frames that last 20 years, 60 years and even 180 years, which is the time it takes for a full nine period cycle of 20 years to complete.

Here in this book, we focus very much on the all-important annual cycles of change, but we also look at the monthly cycles; and we write this book on the basis that we are living through the larger cycle of

Period 8. Broadly speaking, time feng shui takes care of the heavenly cosmic forces that affect the overall trinity of luck.

Finally, there is the self or *spiritual dimension*, which broadly speaking depends on the energies generated by mankind. This focuses on the chi energy individually as well as collectively created by people themselves. How we each individually, and together with others who live with us, empower the energy of self to either create good or bad energy.

In its highest form, the Self energy is believed to be the most powerful of all, and in the face even of extremely challenging **Heaven Luck** as is the case in 2011, the highly empowered self or highly focused person who has the ability to use the powerful forces of his/her mental concentration can indeed generate the all-powerful **Mankind** chi that can subdue afflictions brought by the intangible conflicting energy of the year's forces (**Heaven Luck**) as well as tangible bad energy caused by bad feng shui (**Earth Luck**).

The highly empowered self does not just happen. This too requires learning, practice and experience, and it involves developing a highly focused and concentrated mind that can generate powerful chi. This is **spiritual chi** that takes years to develop, but there are methods - both gross and subtle - that can be used to generate good mankind luck.

These methods are referred to as *inner feng shui*. Traditonal feng shui masters of the old school are great adepts at invoking the Taoist spiritual deities through meditative contemplations and meditations, reciting powerful prayers and mantras and using powerful purification rituals to remove obstacles. Many turn to Buddhist deities who are believed to be very powerful in helping to awaken the inner forces within us. A great deal of feng shui history is thus tied up with Taoism and Buddhist practices in ancient China.

However, this aspect of feng shui is usually kept secret by the Masters, many of whom are also expert at meditation and visualization techniques. It is their meditations that enable them to access their highly empowered inner chi which brings their practice of feng shui to a much higher level of accomplishment.

We found that many of the powerful ancient rituals for overcoming life obstacles, such as those using **incense** and **aromas** and the empowerment of symbolic and holy objects to enhance the spiritual feng shui of homes, found their way to Tibet during the Tang dynasty, where they were incorporated into their spiritual practices, especially those practices that invoked the powerful Protectors of the Land of Snows. These powerful rituals are now being revealed to the world by the high lamas of Tibetan Buddhism. In 2011, it will be especially effective to practice this method of feng shui, as it will alleviate many of the discordant energies of the coming year.

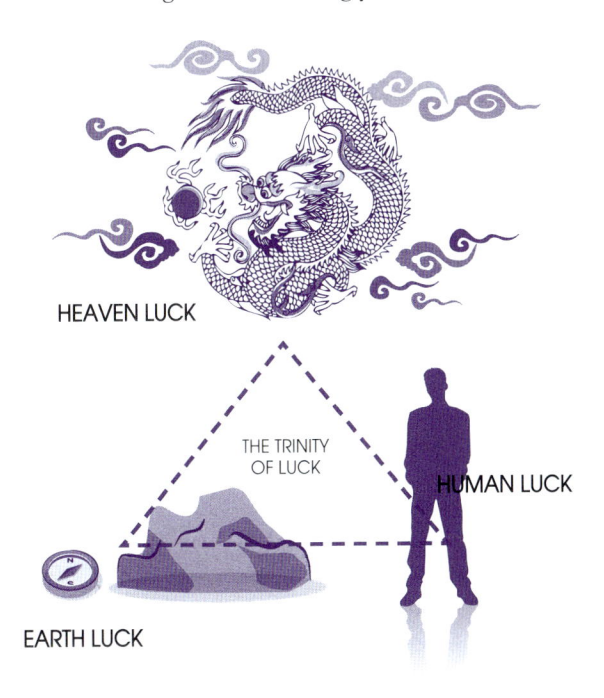

HEAVEN LUCK

THE TRINITY OF LUCK

HUMAN LUCK

EARTH LUCK

Dog Welcomes Auspicious 8 in 2011

- Wood Dog – 77/17 years
- Fire Dog – 65 years
- Earth Dog – 53 years
- Metal Dog – 41 years
- Water Dog – 29 years

Outlook for the Dog In 2011

The Dog sign in 2011 enjoys the Star of 8 in the feng shui chart, so cosmic winds bring excellent prospects and helps to suppress less lucky indications in their element horoscope. These suggest that success quota has been reduced this year, with a downgrading of attainment luck predicted for this year. It therefore benefits Dog to slow down its work pace, and simply go with the flow this year. Allowing the feng shui winds free flow is the best way to reap the fullest benefits of the number 8 star.

In assessing the year, it is helpful to also look at the 24 mountains constellation, which indicates that Dog enjoys the small success star on its left. This tells you that someone of the Boar sign could bring you good fortune. This is interesting, as Boar also belongs to the Northwest sector and has Water in its sign, so this is an important tip to take note of this year.

On the Dog's right is the *three killings* star suggesting some conflict vibes coming from the Rooster on its right. There could be some negativity associated with the Rooster this year. The Dog sign itself is sitting on the star of yearly conflict, which suggest there are envious people who might try to undermine you. They cause obstacles that bring about some aggravation which could lead you to seek diversions or move in a different direction. But this should not be cause to overly worry.

With 8 in your sector, your feng shui energy is strong. You can slow down your rhythm and work pace so that whoever is sending hostility your way will lose the rhythm of your flow. This way, the number 8, whose energy is powerful, has a chance to help you. It will more than make up for the personal energy that is lacking this year. Dog is certain to enjoy at least some small success. Be satisfied with this, as this is not a year to go aggressively chasing after big dreams and ambitions. This is not a year to run too fast. It pays to move slower, at a measured pace, giving yourself time to ponder and savor what comes to you in this decidedly good year.

Health concerns brought by the interaction of your year-of-birth elements with the elements of the year might adversely affect the **65 year old Fire Dog**, although you will have no financial worries. The **17 year old Wood Dog** and **41 year old Metal Dog** enjoy very good health in 2011 with no worries whatsoever. It is however the **29 year old Water Dog** who gets the best of the year's energies, enjoying both excellent wealth and pretty good health luck. Financially, the year works out well for this young up-and-coming person, who is likely to be on the verge of enjoying some big breakthrough in his/her career. This should be a great year for you!

For every one of you belonging to the Dog sign, the year brings some interesting new experiences. The 8 star is an all-encompassing auspicious number and it is also vigorous. Allowing it to ripen should bring new dimensions into your life. Just making time to realise this empowers the good luck to manifest. No need to work like a dog! Instead, leave it to the power of the

8 star. Note that 8 is an Earth star which has natural affinity with Dog whose intrinsic element is also Earth.

The Dog's location falls in the Northwest which is where the powerful Chien trigram resides. With the 8 here, excellent luck ripens for the patriarchs and leaders of the world. It brings noticeable benefits for the male Dog. The main thing to watch out for is potential conflict. The key to an enjoyable and fulfilling year is to simply turn your back on anyone or anything too controversial. Make it a point to actively and consciously avoid conflict situations, and you should sail through the year with enjoyable equanimity.

The Dog Personality in 2011

The Dog sign is a happy sign in 2011. Buoyed aloft by the good feng shui winds of the year, you have the personality to gracefully accept all that the year throws out, warts and all. It enjoys of course the number 8 star, which brings awesome energy to the totally yang Chien trigram. So there is natural wisdom and good humor in the Dog personality.

There could be envious eyes cast your way in 2011 causing some controversy, and conflict can get a little out of hand. But most Dog people are diplomatic and not quick to anger. This is not to suggest you are a pushover; indeed, beware the snarling Dog! It is just that Dog will not have the energy to fight anyone this year, and has no stomach for it either. Since you are skillful at avoiding trouble, it is unlikely that the yearly conflict star in your 24 mountains constellation can cause too much harm.

It is nevertheless important to point out that Dog's Horoscope indications look quite negative and this can bring on bouts of pessimism, despite good news coming your way. The perception of negativity on your part could reduce your good luck. Remember that its all in your mind! Dog rarely if ever blames others, so you tend to carry the whole burden of your own pessimism yourself. It is a good thing that the 8 is here to guard you from being taken advantage of by people who see you for the soft-hearted person you are. In an either-or situation, Dog tends to drag its feet this year, preferring to avoid confronting problem situations directly. This can sometimes bring more good than bad.

Overall however, this is a cheerful year with good news for many of you. Things can go wrong occasionally, caused by relationship difficulties, but by and large, the Dog's personality should see you weave yourself skilfully through the year.

OUTLOOK FOR THE LADY DOG IN 2011

BIRTH YEAR	TYPE OF DOG LADY	LO SHU AT BIRTH	AGE	LUCK OUTLOOK IN 2011
1946	Fire Dog Lady	9	65	Good money luck in auspicious year
1958	Earth Dog Lady	6	53	Small setbacks but year looks good
1970	Metal Dog Lady	3	41	Physical good health brings energy
1982	Water Dog Lady	9	29	An excellent year financially
1994	Wood Dog Lady	6	17	A good gap year maybe?

The Lady Dog continues to go through bouts of pessimism and uncertainty even though there is no real reason to be feeling downcast in any way. It is probably Dog's low Life Force energy and low inner strength that is causing this. In actual fact however, the feng shui winds brought by the year's chart look extremely good indeed. This comes from the number 8 star flying into Dog's Northwest location in 2011.

The lady Dog should shrug her shoulders and welcome the year with a more optimistic outlook. The year starts well and this takes you all the way through Spring. Doubts come only in June but thankfully this is short-lived. There is simply too much to feel good about in 2011.

This is the year of the Rabbit, which is the Dog's secret friend, so it is a friendly year that brings excellent vibes to the Dog sign. Socially, you will find that you are extremely popular and it is likely that social life will take on extremely pleasurable colors this year.

You could also be invited to sit on charitable committees or independent foundations and this gives you new audiences to benefit from your skills and strengths. But it is not necessary to take on too much. The Dog matriarch is better off focusing on family than on the larger community.

Do resist the temptation to put too much on your plate, as 2011 is not the kind of year when you will be terribly appreciated, and community work can sometimes prove to be a thankless task. In fact, it might just add stress to your life, but the 8 star does bring recognition, so you will be called on to serve. Just remember that your horoscope is indicating obstacles to your success luck.

The best tempered woman Dog this year is still the **29 year old Water Dog**, whose career and life seem to be blossoming beautifully. This could turn out to be a benchmark year for you. For the **41 year old Metal lady Dog** health luck stays strong but other indications favour you to take a step backwards and assess the direction your life is taking.

The **65 year old Fire Dog** should not take be taking risks this year. There is good money luck but all indications suggest that it is best not to initiate anything. Leave things to the energy of the year which brings you all the goodies to scoop up. Just make sure to stay optimistic and have positive aspirations, then go with the flow.

OUTLOOK FOR THE GENTLEMAN DOG IN 2011

BIRTH YEAR	TYPE OF DOG MAN	LO SHU AT BIRTH	AGE	LUCK OUTLOOK IN 2011
1946	Fire Dog Man	9	65	Excellent year with financial gains
1958	Earth Dog Man	6	53	Some new challenges coming
1970	Metal Dog Man	3	41	Renewed confidence helps you stay strong
1982	Water Dog Man	9	29	An excellent year financially
1994	Wood Dog Man	6	17	A good gap year maybe?

The gentleman Dog will be in a better frame of mind than his lady counterpart. The man benefits greatly from the number 8 star appearing in the Northwest, especially if he is running his own business, or is a leader or a politician. The luck of the Patriarch is very good this year and for the Dog, the benefits are a certainty, because this is also its home location according to the compass wheel.

On the work front especially, Dog will find there is support and encouragement. The cosmic forces bring good winds, and any effort expended is certain to bring recognition. There could be new challenges and some new opportunity which allow Dog to showcase his skills and talents, as this is a year when the Dog gentleman can find new situations in which to excel.

Your greatest setback could be your lack of staying power. In 2011, your energy is low, so you get stressed more easily. You give in to exhaustion more quickly and there could be a depletion of your inner resources. So the strategy this year is to work at a slower pace. In any case, whatever gains come from working long hours will at best be only marginal. Schedule some down-time to enjoy and relax.

Making progress and moving forward comes from working smart. It is quality of work, not quantity that matters. Dog cannot handle stress well this year. The gentleman Dog has a lovely nature, but at times you might be trying just too hard. This is simply not necessary this year. Better to remain your cool affable self, working at your own pace than make like work is just one long struggle. This way you will not succumb to the negatives of your personal element horoscope.

The **65 year old Fire Dog** has little to worry about as he is in for an excellent year when there is financial improvements to boot. Net worth records a boost. For **53 year old Earth Dog** there are minor health ailments while **41 year old Metal Dog** must cope with setbacks. But there is stability which brings renewed confidence; so on balance, you have a net plus year. The **29 year old Water Dog** guy has the best of all worlds. Money luck is at an all-time high and you can tackle obstacles in other aspects of your life. It is good to go with the flow and to allow feng shui winds to blow good vibes your way.

Going with the Flow in 2011

Success luck for those born under the Dog sign drops drastically from a single X last year to a double XX in your element horoscope chart. This can be considered quite a substantial drop from last year. But you do enjoy other auspicious indications brought by the flying star feng shui chart, and this should assist you to overcome your weak success showing in the element horoscope.

The Dog is sure to feel both sets of energies through the year, so it should not surprise you if you should swing between pessimism and optimism. The lady Dog will be more susceptible to mood swings than the male, but for both, going with the flow is the way to make the best from the year. Accept what 2011 brings and stay positive.

Personal Horoscope Luck in 2011

The horoscope chart of elements for each sign is determined by the heavenly stem element of their year of birth. It shows how their ruling luck elements in their year of birth interact with the luck elements of the year 2011. This interaction reveals if five types of luck are good or bad each year. When the elements of each luck type interact badly with the equivalent elements of 2011, the luck is bad. When it interacts positively, the luck is good.

In 2011, Dog's Life Force continues to be low, registering a double XX, so it is important that this double negative indication be overcome by wearing a spiritual amulet of some kind, perhaps a set of sacred syllables or a talisman that carries multiple repetitions of powerful holy mantras.

An excellent piece of jewellery to wear this wear would be the **Omani Padme Hum prayer wheel pendant** which contains a million mantras in microfilm. This creates powerful protection that will ward off danger of any kind that might be life threatening.

When the wearing of amulets is accompanied by some good deed such as performing animal liberation or donating to some charity, any danger coming to you can be successfully averted. Threats to the Life Force are usually karmic and can be assuaged by a specific kind action on your part.

Unfortunately, Dog's Spirit Essence is equally low, making you vulnerable to the harmful effect of wandering spirits. These spirits exist in a parallel realm alongside humans and many are harmless; they can however be quite vindictive if you unknowingly make them angry; through carelessly saying the wrong things that get picked up by the winds, perhaps desecrating their "homes" such as cutting down old trees or digging up ant hills without properly and ritually seeking permission to do so. These worldly ghosts can only harm those with low Spirit Essence indicated by the double crosses.

The harm usually manifests as illness, which either cannot get cured or keeps persisting, and you might also get weaker. Such indications suggest spirit harm. The cure for this are to recite mantras or perform powerful clearing rituals or pujas and you are unlikely to know how to do this, so the best way is to be protected against spirit harm. The best is to wear some protective talisman or amulet. Wearing decorative jewellery with mantras or sutras inscribed on them will protect you from any spirit harm arising from your vulnerability. It could safeguard you against love charms sent your way by someone who wants you! Also, should anyone out of jealousy use black magic against you, you can get hit because your Spirit Essence is so low. Again, if you wear talismanic protection, you can evade their bad intentions. This is definitely a year for you to be careful.

Other kinds of luck categories according to the element interactions of year 2011 are summarised here. Note that the **Water Dog** and **Fire Dog** enjoy excellent to good financial luck despite success luck being on the low side this year.

Wear jewellery mantras such as this Trinity Ring for protection.

Fire Dog - 65 Years Old

TYPE OF LUCK	ELEMENT AT BIRTH AFFECTING THIS LUCK	ELEMENT IN 2011 AFFECTING THIS LUCK	LUCK RATING
LIFE FORCE	Earth	Wood	XX
HEALTH LUCK	Earth	Wood	XX
FINANCE LUCK	Fire	Metal	OO
SUCCESS LUCK	Metal	Fire	XX
SPIRIT ESSENCE	Fire	Water	XX

HEALTH LUCK - showing XX indicates some serious health ailments afflicting you during the year.

FINANCE LUCK - showing OO indicates some financial gains in your net worth.

SUCCESS LUCK - showing XX indicates a slowing down of success luck.

Earth Dog - 53 Years Old

TYPE OF LUCK	ELEMENT AT BIRTH AFFECTING THIS LUCK	ELEMENT IN 2011 AFFECTING THIS LUCK	LUCK RATING
LIFE FORCE	Earth	Wood	XX
HEALTH LUCK	Wood	Wood	X
FINANCE LUCK	Earth	Metal	OX
SUCCESS LUCK	Metal	Fire	XX
SPIRIT ESSENCE	Fire	Water	XX

HEALTH LUCK - showing X suggests minor health ailments affecting you.

FINANCE LUCK - showing OX indicating some financial loss is possible.

SUCCESS LUCK - showing XX indicating a slowing down of success luck..

Metal Dog - 41 Years Old

TYPE OF LUCK	ELEMENT AT BIRTH AFFECTING THIS LUCK	ELEMENT IN 2011 AFFECTING THIS LUCK	LUCK RATING
LIFE FORCE	Earth	Wood	XX
HEALTH LUCK	Metal	Wood	OO
FINANCE LUCK	Metal	Metal	X
SUCCESS LUCK	Metal	Fire	XX
SPIRIT ESSENCE	Fire	Water	XX

HEALTH LUCK - showing OO suggests that physically you should have no problems.

FINANCE LUCK - showing X indicating that financially, it is not a great year.

SUCCESS LUCK - showing XX indicating a slowing down of success luck.

Water Dog - 29 Years Old

TYPE OF LUCK	ELEMENT AT BIRTH AFFECTING THIS LUCK	ELEMENT IN 2011 AFFECTING THIS LUCK	LUCK RATING
LIFE FORCE	Earth	Wood	XX
HEALTH LUCK	Water	Wood	OX
FINANCE LUCK	Water	Metal	OOO
SUCCESS LUCK	Metal	Fire	XX
SPIRIT ESSENCE	Fire	Water	XX

HEALTH LUCK - showing OX indicates you are in fairly good health with few ailments.

FINANCE LUCK - showing OOO means financial luck is excellent for you.

SUCCESS LUCK - showing XX indicating a slowing down of success luck.

Wood Dog - 17 Years Old

TYPE OF LUCK	ELEMENT AT BIRTH AFFECTING THIS LUCK	ELEMENT IN 2011 AFFECTING THIS LUCK	LUCK RATING
LIFE FORCE	Earth	Wood	XX
HEALTH LUCK	Fire	Wood	OOO
FINANCE LUCK	Wood	Metal	XX
SUCCESS LUCK	Metal	Fire	XX
SPIRIT ESSENCE	Fire	Water	XX

HEALTH LUCK - showing OOO suggests you are in the pink of health this year.

FINANCE LUCK - showing XX indicates some financial loss is possible this year

SUCCESS LUCK - showing XX indicating a slowing down of success luck.

Discover Your Lunar Mansion

How Your Sky Animal Affects Your Luck

Your Lunar Mansion is named one of 28 Sky Animals that pinpoint the Day of the Week that is favorable for you, and more importantly, it reveals what sky constellation you belong to, thereby opening up a mine of information as to the kind of people you work best with; the area of work that offers the best potential for success; and the nature of the assistance your Sky Animal brings you in any given year. Your Lunar Mansion is an integral part of you, so it deepens your understanding of what makes you tick, and how it modifies the attitude tendencies and outlook for your Zodiac sign.

There are four Sky Constellations under each of which are seven Sky Animals, three of them primary and four, secondary.

Those of you born in a Dog year will work well with Sky Animals belonging to the Western Skies, and as a team or partnership, they attract good business luck. At the same time, your own Sky Animal will likewise determine which of other Sky Animals work well with you. Basically, these are colleagues belonging to the same constellation as you.

Each constellation refers to one of four sections of the Skies, which are associated with the Four Celestial Guardians, the Green Dragon who guards the Eastern skies, the Crimson Phoenix who protects the Southern Skies, the Black Tortoise Lord of the Northern Skies and the White Tiger who rules the Western Skies.

The Celestials and the Sky Animals mirror the Celestial Guardians of feng shui and the Zodiac animal signs that make up the earthly branches of astrology. This mirror effect strengthens specific types of good fortune. Sky Animals rarely bring obstacles as their effect is generally positive. They signify the influence of heaven.

Lucky Day

Everyone is born on a DAY that corresponds to one of these Sky Animals. In astrological terms, this is the lucky DAY for you. It is described as your corresponding Lunar Mansion and it reveals the influence of star constellations on your professional and business life from year to year. One's lunar mansion is analyzed in conjunction with one's personal Four Pillars chart and the Four Pillars chart of the year. Such a detailed analysis is not within the scope of this book, but it is useful to know the trends brought by the influence of your Lunar Mansion (or Sky Animal) in terms of your relationships and your luck in 2011.

Compatibility

For instance, everyone belonging to the same constellation and coming under the same Celestial Guardian has an affinity with each other, and in times of trouble, one can depend on the other, sometimes even in spite of them being opposing signs based on year of birth.

Sky Animals also have natural affinity to their corresponding Zodiac animal signs e.g. a Sky Dog has affinity with someone born in the year of the Dog and vice versa. A Sky Dog will also have affinity with someone born in the year of the Tiger or Horse (Dog's allies). This applies for all 12 animal Zodiac signs, as each sign has a Sky counterpart!

Meanwhile, you can also be a secret friend of a Sky Animal. Thus the Sky Rabbit is the secret friend of the Dog. This creates very powerful work luck, as your heaven and earth chi blend well. This is a heaven and earth relationship. In itself, this is an indication of auspicious chi, so it is good for the Dog to go into partnership with someone who is a Sky Rabbit.

Determining the Dominant Celestial Guardian

The coming year 2011 is a Rabbit Year with two Tigers and a Horse in its Pillars chart. This suggests that the Green Dragon who rules the Eastern Skies is dominant. This arises from it being a Rabbit Year and the Rabbit is one of the Sky signs belonging to the Dragon constellation. The Dragon rules the Skies of the East and included in this constellation are also the Sky Tiger. The Zodiac Tiger whose location is part of the East also makes appearances in the year's paht chee. The strength and influence of the Dragon's constellation is thus very powerful in 2011. It is definitely beneficial to invite the image of the Dragon into the home in 2011.

Note especially that in 2011, the lunar year begins on the **3rd of February** which corresponds to the day before the lap chun, the day of Spring. This is an auspicious indication. This could bring miracles to the year and help in transforming conflict energy into something productive.

With the Dragon as the ruling celestial guardian, growth energy during the year will be strong. The Sky Dragon is the key to subduing all discordant energies brought by the clashing elements on earth.

Lining up all seven animals of the Dragon's constellation is believed to bring greater strength for getting projects started and attracting the good fortune of the Sky Dragon constellation. This applies to the Rabbit, its seasonal ally, the Dragon, as well as to those born in the sign of the Tiger.

Even just placing the three main Sky signs of this constellation - the Dragon, Tiger and Rabbit - would be extremely auspicious and it benefits to place them in the East part of your garden or along an East wall of your living room. Sky signs look exactly like their Zodiac counterparts.

Green Dragon Constellation

The seven Sky Animals that belong to the Dragon's constellation of the Eastern skies are the Sky Dragon, Sky Rabbit and Sky Tiger, as well as the Sky Salamander, Beaver, Fox and Leopard.

1. The Sky Salamander

This sky creature epitomizes the phenomenon of growth energy, associated mainly with agriculture and plantations. Any kind of profession associated with plants, gardens or plantations would be beneficial. This creature has no affinity with the Dog and it is a cousin of the Dragon. If this is your Lunar Mansion, your creative instincts could conflict with your natural inclinations. Your lucky day is Thursday.

2. The Sky Dragon

This powerful creature is said to be a magician, able to create wondrous things out of nothing more than dreams. Success comes early in life and you could peak earlier than you wish. The Dog born with this sign finds strength in pursuing its own ideas and operating with high confidence. You can take some risks this year and there could be big things coming your way in 2011. Stay relaxed! Your lucky day is Friday.

3. The Sky Beaver
This is a creature that signifies stability and good foundation. If this is your sign, you should seek out mentors, people senior to you who could bring you *"follow my leader luck"*. A Dog born with this Sky Animal sign usually benefits significantly, because the Sky Beaver enhances your networking skills and these open pathways to many lucrative opportunities. Your lucky day is Saturday.

4. The Sky Rabbit
This is the most accommodating creature of this Constellation, usually associated with bringing family members together and establishing the bliss of domestic comforts. A Dog born with this sign will put family above work in 2011. Your lucky day is Sunday.

5. The Sky Fox
This crafty, alert and quick-witted creature could be at odds with the Dog's nature, so this is rarely a good combination, although it can bring

success. Described as the heart and soul of the Dragon constellation, this creature can steer Dog to go against its instincts, and rightly or wrongly, help you reach an influential and high position. Your lucky day is Monday.

6. The Sky Tiger

This is the creature is said to be born with a jade pendant on its forehead; so power and authority comes naturally to anyone who is a Sky Tiger. Success can be assured in the political arena and they also receive unexpected windfalls of luck all through their life, attracting help and support from family and friends. The Dog works well with this sign. Your lucky day is Tuesday.

7. The Sky Leopard

This is the creature that benefits from being close to the Dragon; the wind beneath the sails, the faithful second in command. Sky leopards are almost always surrounded by many of the good things in life whether or not these belong to them. Nevertheless they are able to enjoy life's luxuries. The Dog born as a Sky Leopard can achieve success if they are discreet, loyal and keep their own counsel. Your lucky day is Wednesday.

Black Tortoise Constellation

For the Dog born, if your Sky Animal comes under the Tortoise constellation, you personify the good life with little effort. This creates energies that make it easy for you to take the fullest advantage of your good fortune indications in 2011. It becomes a double bonus this year. The animals of the Tortoise Constellation are the Sky Ox (NE1), the Sky Rat (North), and the Sky Boar (NW3). There are also the Sky Unicorn, the Sky Bat, the Sky Swallow and the Sky Porcupine.

8. The Sky Unicorn
This creature combines the speed of the Horse with the courage of the Dragon. For the Dog, if this is your Sky Animal, it indicates two extreme sides of you, for the Unicorn is at once your best friend and your own worst enemy. Dog born people whose Sky counterpart is the Unicorn could have an exaggerated sense of do-goodness about them. You have to look beyond small grievances and take the big picture approach to attaining all your dreams. Make sure you do not lose out on the main chance. Your lucky day is Thursday.

9. The Sky Ox

This creature is associated with the legend of the weaving maiden and the Ox boy forced to live apart and able to meet only once a year. Dog born people whose Sky Animal is the Ox will enjoy favorable luck in 2011, especially in real estate investments. The single Dog could also find true love this year, but there may be small obstacles. Your lucky day is Friday.

10. The Sky Bat

This is a secondary sign of the Tortoise constellation but is a symbol that signifies extreme good fortune. Benefits keep coming to you, especially if you are in the construction or engineering profession. Dog people with this Sky sign enjoy a life of comfort, living in a mansion through adult life. The Bat is greatly blessed if living in a temple or turns spiritual. There is good fortune awaiting you in 2011. Your lucky day is Saturday.

11. The Sky Rat

This sign signifies winter where yin energy rules. Dogs whose Sky sign is the Sky Rat enjoy auspicious luck brought by 2011. A very auspicious year awaits you.

You will be on the receiving end of some good fortune. Your lucky day is Sunday.

12. The Sky Swallow
This is the sign often associated with foolhardiness and danger as the swallow flies too fast and too high. This is the risk taker of the Tortoise constellation. Dog born people having this Sky sign tend to be extra impulsive, rushing into making decisions without thinking through. If this is your sign, do reflect carefully before committing to anything new. Your lucky day is Monday.

13. The Sky Boar
This is a sign associated with the good life which gets better as you get older. Dog born people having this Sky sign are likely to be living in a mansion. You will enjoy good fortune in 2011 and the older you are, the better the luck coming your way. Good year to move into a bigger house. Your lucky day is Tuesday.

14. The Sky Porcupine
This is the policeman of this constellation, always conscious of security, alert to people with dishonest intentions. Dog born people having this sign are artistic and hardworking,

and very committed to what they do. This is a year when you can excel. Do not lose confidence in yourself in 2011, otherwise you might not have the courage to accept what comes your way. Your lucky day is Wednesday.

White Tiger Constellation

The White Tiger constellation tends to be vulnerable in 2011, hence those born into this grouping are advised to take things easy and lie low. The mountain stars affecting the Western skies are potentially disastrous, bringing misfortune. Taking risks could be dangerous and the year itself already shows several warning signs, so it is best not to be too adventurous or foolhardy.

The Dog whose Sky Animal falls under this constellation should be alert to warning signs. It is beneficial to take the conciliatory approach at all times. Also, discretion is the better part of valor and it is better to be safe than sorry. This is not a good year for Sky Animals in this constellation to take unnecessary risks.

The Tiger's constellation has the Sky Dog (NW1), the Sky Rooster (West) and the Sky Monkey (SW3). On a compass, you can see this reflects the Western skies sector. These are creatures of Autumn, when others are preparing to hibernate. In 2011, when the year is dangerous for this grouping of Sky Animals, it is a good time to stay less active.

The secondary Sky Animals of the Tiger Constellation - the Sky Wolf, Sky Pheasant, Sky Raven and Sky Ape - protect and support the main creatures with all seven coming under the care of the White Tiger. In astrological terms, the signs in the grouping of the Western Sky creatures are the most commercially-minded of all the Sky Animals. In 2011, protection is the keyword for those belonging to this constellation.

15. The Sky Wolf
This is an insecure creature with a tendency towards negativity, expecting the worse to happen. The Sky Wolf requires plenty of reassurance and it is this lack of confidence that is its worst drawback. A Dog who is a Sky Wolf must exert efforts to stay upbeat, especially in 2011. Confidence is the key to succeeding. Your lucky day is Thursday.

16. The Sky Dog
This is an excellent sky sign as it indicates a life of success. The Sky Dog always has a pile of treasures at its feet; commercial

and business success comes easily and effortlessly and theirs is a life filled with celebration and merry making. The Dog who is also a Sky Dog can find success in 2011 benefiting from the stars of *Big Auspicious*. But you have conflicting emotions and you need to be careful this year. Your lucky day is Friday.

17. The Sky Pheasant

This is another good Sky sign as the Pheasant indicates someone successful at creating and keeping their wealth. This is a Sky sign that is particularly suited to a career involving finance such as banking. This sign will also never be short of money as the Sky Pheasant attracts wealth continuously. A Dog with this sign is sure to be rich but do be alert to anyone trying to con you of your money this year! Your lucky day is Saturday.

18. The Sky Rooster

This creature reflects its Zodiac counterpart, being naturally vigilant and watchful. The Sky Rooster is described as the eyes and ears of the skies ever alert to those who would disturb the natural order. You are an excellent one to have around in 2011 which is a year when your instincts are at their most alert. Dog born with this Sky sign will be going through risky but potentially prosperous times. Your lucky day is Sunday.

19. The Sky Raven
This is the creature of the Sky that signifies extremely rich rewards from efforts expended. The Sky Raven is associated with success of the most outstanding kind. As long as you are determined enough, you will get what you work for. Be mindful of the year's sudden obstacles and you can negotiate through the pitfalls. The Dog born with this sign will need to work hard and be alert. Your lucky day is Monday.

20. The Sky Monkey
This is a natural born leader who assumes leadership responsibilities without hesitation, naturally extending protective arms outwards. They are thus charismatic and attractive. A Dog born with the sign of the Sky Monkey will be a role model of some kind. Others are inspired by you. Your lucky day is Tuesday.

21. The Sky Ape
This is the creature that signifies the important law of karma, ripening for them faster than for others. Thus the Sky Ape succeeds when they work and find life

difficult when they slack off. Good deeds bring instant good rewards and likewise also vile deeds. A Dog with this Sky sign will have good instincts in 2011. Your lucky day is Wednesday.

Crimson Phoenix Constellation

The Crimson Phoenix rules the Southern skies and its Sky Animals are the Sky Horse (South), Sky Sheep (SW1), and Sky Snake (SE3). As with the creatures of the other constellations, any family or business entity represented by this group of Sky Animals under the Phoenix benefit each other immensely. Collectively they attract exciting opportunities; their best time comes during the summer months and working on weekends benefits them. The Sky Animals or Lunar Mansions of the Southern skies are:

22. The Sky Anteater

This is a creature that has the potential to exert great influence, but whether or not this can materialize depends on other factors. The Sky Anteater can be a catalyst, but it cannot initiate or spearhead a project or be a leader. But as someone supporting someone else, there is no better person. Dog born with this Sky sign will work better from behind the scenes. Your lucky day is Thursday.

23. The Sky Sheep
This Sky sign indicates someone who will eventually become deeply spiritual or psychic. When developed to its fullest potential, such a person becomes incredibly charismatic - easily becoming an iconic source of inspiration to others. A Dog born with this Sky sign can achieve brilliance in business or politics. Your lucky day is Friday.

24. The Sky Roebuck
This is a creature of healing, someone who has the gift to mend broken hearts and emotionally distraught people. Those with this Sky sign have calm dispositions ,so a Dog born under this Sky sign is an excellent calming influence on anyone. This sign can be a counselor. Your lucky day is Saturday.

25. The Sky Horse

This is a lovely Sky sign loved by many people. Also referred to as the mediator of the skies, the Sky Horse takes everyone for a joyride, helping others forget their grievances with great effectiveness. A Dog born with this sign tends to be adventurous. Your lucky day is Sunday.

26. The Sky Deer

This is a generous creature whose spirit of giving endears it to many others. The Sky Deer is often also associated with those who make it to a high position and then using their influence and success to benefit many others. A Dog who has this Sky sign is sure to have this beautiful dimension of generosity in their personality. Your lucky day is Monday.

27. The Sky Snake

This creature represents imperial authority. The Sky Snake travels on the wings of the Phoenix, always ready to receive the applause and adoration of others. Sky Snakes enjoy the destiny of personal advancement, especially in the political arena. A Dog who is a Sky Snake should benefit in 2011. Your lucky day is Tuesday.

28. The Sky Worm

Humble as this creature may sound, the Sky Worm aims high, and when it succeeds, it does so with panache and great style. This is the great surprise of the constellation of lunar mansions because those born under this sign have great perseverance and amazing courage to take risks; success for them comes with a vengeance! The Dog with this sign should do well in 2011. Your lucky day is Wednesday.

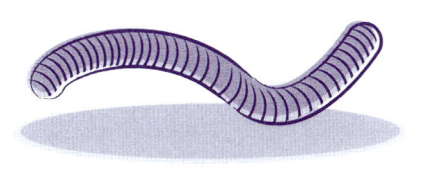

Determining Your Sky Animal Sign

Example: If your day of birth is
18th July 1970

1. Get the corresponding number for your **month** and **year** from **Table 1**. Thus the number for **July** is **12**, and the number for the year **1970** is **8**.

2. Next, add the numbers of the month and the year to the day is **18**. Thus 12 + 8 + 18 = **38**.

3. Next determine if your year of birth **1970** is a leap year; if it is, and you were born **after** March 1st, add 1. Here 1970 is not a leap year and you were born after **March 1st**, so here you do not add 1 to **38** so it stays **38**.

4. As **38** is lower than **56** but higher than 28, you need to subtract 28 from 52. Thus **38 - 28 = 10.** So note that for you, the Sky Animal is number **10**.

To explain this part of the calculation note that since there are 28 animals, any number higher than 28 should deduct 28 and any number higher than 56 which is 28 x 2, should deduct 56 from the total to reach a number that is lower than 28. **This will indicate your Lunar Mansion number.**

Once you have your number, which in this example is 10, your Sky Animal (or Lunar Mansion) is the one corresponding to the number 10 in Table 2.

In this example of someone born on 18th July 1970, your Sky Animal is the **Sky Bat** and you belong to the Constellation of the **Black Tortoise** of the Southern skies. Your lucky day is Sunday and you belong to the constellation season of Winter.

Meanwhile, based on your year of birth, you are born under the Zodiac sign of the **Metal Dog**.

TABLE 1
To Determine the Animal of Your Day of Birth

MONTH	YEAR	YEAR	YEAR	YEAR	YEAR	NO.
-	1920*	1942	-	1987	2009	1
FEB, MAR	-	1943	1965	1988*	2010	2
-	1921	1944*	1966	-	2011	3
-	1922	-	1967	1989	2012*	4
APRIL	1923	1945	1968*	1990	-	5
-	1924*	1946	-	1991	2013	6
MAY	-	1947	1969	1992*	2014	7
-	1925	1948*	1970	-	2015	8
-	1926	-	1971	1993	2016*	9
JUNE	1927	1949	1972*	1994	-	10
-	1928*	1950	-	1995	2017	11
JULY	-	1951	1973	1996*	2018	12
-	1929	1952*	1974	-	2019	13
-	1930	-	1975	1997	2020*	14
AUGUST	1931	1953	1976*	1998	-	15
-	1932*	1954	-	1999	2021	16
-	-	1955	1977	2000*	2022	17
SEPTEMBER	1933	1956*	1978	-	2023	18
-	1934	-	1979	2001	2024*	19
OCTOBER	1935	1957	1980*	2002	-	20
-	1936*	1958	-	2003	2025	21
-	-	1959	1981	2004*	2026	22
NOVEMBER	1937	1960*	1982	-	2027	23
-	1938	-	1983	2005	2028*	24
DECEMBER	1939	1961	1984*	2006	-	25
-	1940*	1962	-	2007	2029	26
JANUARY	-	1963	1985	2008*	2030	27
-	1941	1964*	1986	-	2031	28

* indicates a leap year

TABLE 2
The 28 Animals of the Four Constellations

**FAMILY OF THE GREEN DRAGON
RULING THE SEASON OF SPRING**

Lunar Mansion Constellations of the **Eastern** skies

1. **Sky Salamander** THURSDAY
2. **Sky Dragon** FRIDAY
3. **Sky Beaver** SATURDAY
4. **Sky Rabbit** SUNDAY
5. **Sky Fox** MONDAY
6. **Sky Tiger** TUESDAY
7. **Sky Leopard** WEDNESDAY

**FAMILY OF THE BLACK TORTOISE
RULING THE SEASON OF WINTER**

Lunar Mansion Constellations of the **Northern** skies

8. **Sky Unicorn** THURSDAY
9. **Sky Ox** FRIDAY
10. **Sky Bat** SATURDAY
11. **Sky Rat** SUNDAY
12. **Sky Swallow** MONDAY
13. **Sky Boar** TUESDAY
14. **Sky Porcupine** WEDNESDAY

**FAMILY OF THE WHITE TIGER
RULING THE SEASON OF AUTUMN**

Lunar Mansion Constellations of the **Western** skies

15. **Sky Wolf** THURSDAY
16. **Sky Dog** FRIDAY
17. **Sky Pheasant** SATURDAY
18. **Sky Rooster** SUNDAY
19. **Sky Raven** MONDAY
20. **Sky Monkey** TUESDAY
21. **Sky Ape** WEDNESDAY

**FAMILY OF THE CRIMSON PHOENIX
RULING THE SEASON OF SUMMER**

Lunar Mansion Constellations of the **Southern** skies

22. **Sky Ant Eater** THURSDAY
23. **Sky Sheep** FRIDAY
24. **Sky Antler** SATURDAY
25. **Sky Horse** SUNDAY
26. **Sky Deer** MONDAY
27. **Sky Snake** TUESDAY
28. **Sky Worm** WEDNESDAY

Interacting With Others In 2011

Part 4

Your Excellent Feng Shui Winds Hide Your Vulnerability

Many things affect how one animal sign gets along with another and the Chinese believe that much of this has to do with astrological forces and influences of a particular year. The varying factors result in a difference in compatibility levels each year and while it is impossible to take note of everything, the key variables to note are one's chi energy essence and whether the year's constellations are making you feel positive and good about yourself. The influence of the YEAR on the compatibilities of relationships is thus important; you cannot ignore the annual chi effect on the way you interact with your loved ones and family.

New energies influence the way you treat people, in turn determining how they respond to you. How you interact with close friends and loved ones is affected by your mental and physical state. So how you get on with your partner, your spouse, parents, children, siblings, relatives and friends are affected by your fortunes in any given year. But relationships are important because how these work out create important inputs to your happiness.

Understanding compatibility makes you more understanding; when differences crop up, these need not be taken to heart. Good vibes make you tolerant while afflictive energies and negative stars suffered by others can make them seem tiresome.

Annual energy also influences what kind of people you will have greater or lesser affinity with. In some years you might feel an inexplicable aversion to someone you may always have liked and loved; or be attracted to someone you have always found annoying! Usually of course, the affinity groupings, secret friends alliances and ideal soul mate pairings of the Zodiac exert strong influences too, but annual chi plays a dominant role in swaying your thinking and those of others. They can make you more argumentative or make you more loving.

People tend to be more or less tolerant or selfish, cold or warm depending on the way things turn out for them from year to year. When life and work goes well, we become better disposed towards others. Then, even a natural zodiac enemy can become a soulmate, if only for a short period of time. Likewise, when one is being challenged by big problems, even the slightest provocation can lead to anger. Zodiac friends and allies might even then appear to be insufferable. A falling out between horoscope allies is thus not impossible.

In this section, we examine the Dog's personal relationships with the other eleven signs in 2011.

Zodiac Influences
1. Alliance of Allies
2. Zodiac Soulmates
3. Secret Friends
4. Astrology Enemies
5. Peach Blossom
6. Seasonal Trinity

1. Alliance of Allies

Four affinity groupings of animal signs form an Alliance of natural allies in the Horoscope. The three signs possess similar thought processes and aspirations and share similar goals. They support each other and can be depended on.

When all three signs enjoy good fortune in any year, it makes the alliance strong, and if there is an alliance within a family unit, such as amongst siblings, or with the spouses and their child, the family is extremely supportive, giving strength to each other. In good years, auspicious luck gets multiplied. Allies always get along. Any falling out is temporary. They trust each other and close ranks against external threats. Good astrological feng shui comes from carrying the image of your allies, especially when they are going through good years.

ALLY GROUPINGS	ANIMALS	CHARACTERISTICS
COMPETITORS	Rat, Dragon, Monkey	Competent, Tough, Resolute
INTELLECTUALS	Ox, Snake, Rooster	Generous, Focused, Resilient
ENTHUSIASTS	**Dog, Tiger, Horse**	**Aggressive, Rebellious, Coy**
DIPLOMATS	Boar, Sheep, Rabbit	Creative, Kind, Emotional

Part 4 : Interacting with Others in 2011

The Dog and its allies as a group will find that it is Dog who is the strongest in the alliance in 2011 in terms of enjoying good fortune, although element-wise, Dog is weak, but here its allies, especially the Horse, brings great support. The phenomenon of the alliance of allies is precisely for those who understand it to get support from each other, so that as a group, you can weather the storms of a challenging year more successfully. Indeed, when the alliance cooperate with each other and team up, their collective energy will get magnified.

Hence if your business associates and you comprise this grouping of Dog, Horse and Tiger, you can take better advantage of your great good fortune this year. If there are three of you in a family, or within the same department of a company, the alliance can be activated to benefit every member.

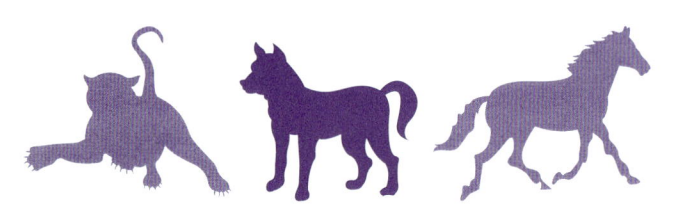

The Tiger, Dog and Horse are horoscope allies of the Chinese Zodiac.

In this alliance, you, the Dog, can lead in 2011. Although afflicted by the yearly conflict star, you have enough good winds to pull you through on whatever you set your mind to.

The Dog is also the diplomat in this alliance, being less volatile and explosive than its two allies, the Tiger and the Horse! In 2011, Dog enjoys the luck of the auspicious star 8, so despite its weak chi essence, Dog is a very significant and vital component of this action-oriented Alliance.

2. Zodiac Soulmates

Six pairs of animal signs create six Zodiac Houses of yin and yang soulmates. Each pair creates powerful bonding at a cosmic level. Marriages or business unions between people belonging to the same Zodiac House are extremely auspicious. In a marriage, there is promise of great happiness. In a commercial partnership, it promises wealth and success. This pairing is good between professional colleagues and siblings.

The strength of each pair is different; with their own defining strength, and with some making better commercial than marriage partners. How successful you are as a pair depends on how you bond. The table here summarizes the key strength of each Zodiac house.

HOUSES OF PAIRED SOULMATES

ANIMALS	YIN/YANG	ZODIAC HOUSE OF CREATIVITY	TARGET UNLEASHED
Rat	YANG	HOUSE OF CREATIVITY & CLEVERNESS	The Rat initiates
Ox	YIN		The Ox completes
Tiger	YANG	HOUSE OF GROWTH & DEVELOPMENT	The Tiger employs force
Rabbit	YIN		The Rabbit uses diplomacy
Dragon	YANG	HOUSE OF MAGIC & SPRITITUALITY	The Dragon creates magic
Snake	YIN		The Snake creates mystery
Horse	YANG	HOUSE OF PASSION & SEXUALITY	The Horse embodies male energy
Sheep	YIN		The Sheep is the female energy
Monkey	YANG	HOUSE OF CAREER & COMMERCE	The Monkey creates strategy
Rooster	YIN		The Rooster get things moving
Dog	YANG	HOUSE OF DOMESTICITY	The Dog works to provide
Boar	YIN		The Boar enjoys what is created

A coming together of yang Dog with its soulmate the yin Boar creates the House of Domesticity. It is a very lovely alliance that as a team generates wonderful family harmony because these are two animal signs for whom domestic bliss is more important than anything else. Family is extremely important to you, so the bond you share is very strong and powerfully loyal. A marriage between the two of you is certain to be very harmonious and happy. And note that this is going to be such an excellent year for you both!

3. Secret Friends

There are six sets of a *secret friendship* that exists between the animal signs of the Zodiac. Between them a very powerful affinity exists making them excellent for each other. Love, respect and goodwill flow freely between secret friends; and they create wonderful happiness vibes for each other in a marriage. Once forged, it is a bond that is hard to break; and even when they themselves want to break, it will be hard for either party to fully walk away. This pair of signs will stick together through thick and thin.

In the pairing of secret friends, the Dog is paired with the Rabbit. There is a bond between these two animal signs and in spite of their different personalities, they stay loyal to one another. The Rabbit does not have the same depth of commitment that Dog people have, but they are soulmates nevertheless. A marriage between them promises happiness and harmony as both are amiable people for whom giving in is never a problem.

PAIRINGS OF SECRET FRIENDS

🐀	Rat	Ox	🐂
🐖	Boar	Tiger	🐅
🐕	**Dog**	**Rabbit**	🐇
🐉	Dragon	Rooster	🐓
🐍	Snake	Monkey	🐒
🐎	Horse	Sheep	🐐

4. Astrological Enemies

Then there are the astrological enemies of the Horoscope. This is the sign that directly confronts yours in the Astrology Compass.

For the Dog, the enemy is the Dragon. Note that the enemy does not necessarily harm you; it only means someone of this sign can never be of any real help to you. Both animal signs belong to the Earth element. This suggests that their animosity does not go as deep as between some of the other astrological foes. There is a six year gap between the two signs and any pairing between them is unlikely to benefit either side. They cannot have sincere intentions towards one another.

PAIRINGS OF ASTROLOGICAL ENEMIES

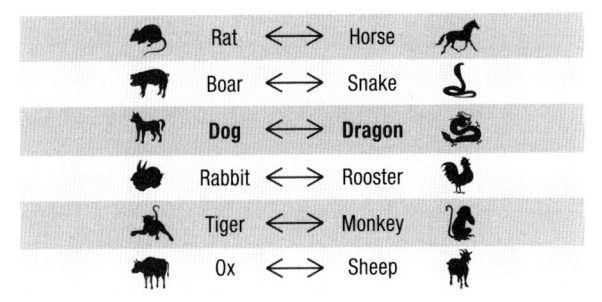

Rat	⟷	Horse
Boar	⟷	Snake
Dog	⟷	**Dragon**
Rabbit	⟷	Rooster
Tiger	⟷	Monkey
Ox	⟷	Sheep

Marriage between a Dog and Dragon may last but is unlikely to bring enduring happiness unless there are other indications in their respective paht chee charts. Pairings between arrows of antagonism are better discouraged. Dog people are advised to refrain from getting involved with a Dragon.

As a business partnership, the pairing is likely to lead to problems, and in the event of a split, the separation can be acrimonious even if they start out as the best of friends. In 2010, any coming together of the Dog and the Dragon will not be a good idea. There will be betrayal and acrimonious quarrels between them. However in 2011, the Dog is feeling generous to the world and thus has greater patience, even with the Dragon.

Nevertheless, when two opposite signs have a hostile astrological connections, they are better off not staying in the same house as there is sure to be trouble and misunderstandings. If they are siblings, they will eventually drift apart. Better for them to stay apart… then at least there won't be direct antagonism.

5. Peach Blossom Links

Each of the Alliance of Allies has a special relationship with one of the four primary signs of Horse, Rat, Rooster and Rabbit in that these are the symbolic representations of love and romance for one Alliance group of animal signs. In the Horoscope, they are referred to as peach blossom animals and the presence of their images in the homes of the matching Alliance of Allies brings peach blossom luck which is associated with love and romance.

The Dog belongs to the Dog, Horse and Tiger alliance, and the Rabbit is their peach blossom link. The Dog will benefit from associating with anyone born in the Rabbit year, and will also benefit from placing a painting or image of a Rabbit in the East corner of the house, or in the Dog direction of Northwest.

5. Seasonal Trinity

Another grouping of animal signs creates the four seasonal trinity combinations that bring the luck of seasonal abundance. To many astrology experts, this is regarded as one of the most powerful combinations, and when it exists within a family made up of either parent or both parents) and with one or more children, it indicates that, collectively these family members are strong enough to transform all negative luck indications for the family members that make up the combination for the entire year.

Thus when the annual indications of the year are not favorable, the existence of the seasonal combination of animal signs in any living abode can transform the bad luck into better luck especially during the season indicated by the combination.

SEASONAL TRINITIES OF THE HOROSCOPE

ANIMAL SIGNS	SEASON	ELEMENT	DIRECTION
Dragon, Rabbit, Tiger	Spring	Wood	East
Snake, Horse, Sheep	Summer	Fire	South
Monkey, Rooster, Dog	**Autumn**	**Metal**	**West**
Ox, Rat, Boar	Winter	Water	North

All three signs must live together in the same house or be in the same office working in close proximity for this powerful pattern to work well. For greater impact, it is better feng shui if they are all using the direction associated with the relevant seasons. The table below summarises the Seasonal groupings.

The Dog belongs to the seasonal combination of Autumn, a combination which creates harmonious and auspicious links with the Rooster and the Monkey, two animal signs that are excellent as business partners. They are sure to benefit Dog should they both be present in the life of the Dog person. When Dog and Monkey marry for instance and they have a Rooster child, the three of them form the trinity of Autumn.

This means that they are not only exceptionally close astrologically (especially towards the third quarter of the year) but they also attract truly incredible luck of the Autumn months! Here, Monkey and Rooster will make the money while Dog will look after the domestic side of their life.

The Monkey, Rooster and Dog make up the seasonal combination of Autumn.

Part 4 : Interacting with Others in 2011

DOG WITH RAT
Enduring conflicts through the year

The Dog who gets involved with someone born in the year of the Rat will find the year's energies simply too difficult to cope with. This is because while other signs may soothe Rat's impatient tendencies, Dog will uncharacteristically respond and if necessary even retaliate. The year sees those born in the year of the Dog becoming more aggressive so it is important not to make Dog an adversary. Despite any tendency to become loud and quarrelsome, Rat is well advised to take a deep breath and not rile Dog.

Astrological signs for the year indicate a happy but rather conflicted time for Dog. There are many things to cope with despite its life force and chi essence being weak; it is a year when Dog is visited by the *Star of Yearly Conflict* so there will be political problems rearing its ugly head.

The Dog born is flanked by the *Star of Small Auspicious* on one side and the *three killings* on the other. Dog needs to exercise patience as much as Rat, and in fact can take the lead in not allowing both their egos to get out of hand. As long as Rat plays fair and does not indulge in hitting below the belt, this couple can come through the year stronger and wiser.

Two Egos Confronting ♥♥♥

Dog is a fiercely loyal friend and even more loyal lover. Rat can be righteous but is also loyal. So while their problems could cause them to have very short fuses in 2011, to the outside world, Rat and Dog will always present a united front. They rarely give out the slightest hint of there being anything wrong between them.

In this sense, Rat and Dog build a world all their own. They can lead separate lives even while living together should the need arise. Dog is good at keeping its cool in the face of difficulties and while it may bark and wail, Dog is actually a lot better at staying firm and in control than Rat. In 2011, this trait shows itself clearly and happily, Rat will play along Dog to take the lead in their relationship.

For the **27 year old Wood Rat** and **29 year old Water Dog**, the year brings much better luck to Rat but greater strength to Dog. In 2011, Dog's financial luck looks good. The elements of the two signs balance well, so there is harmony for this pair. For the **39 year old Water Rat** and the **41 year old Metal Dog**, the elements favor Rat, although both have well balanced horoscope luck.

DOG WITH OX
Ups and downs through a jolly year

The Ox in 2011 will find in Dog an amazing and attractive friend to do things with. This is not a naturally compatible pair, but the energy that surrounds these two signs in 2011 is conducive to creating an excellent time together. As a couple, they will see and bring out the best in one another. This comes from their personal chi energy brought by the forces of some truly excellent feng shui winds. As a result, there is harmony and goodwill flowing freely between this pair.

> Dog and Ox do not have a wildly passionate love affair. Theirs is a restrained relationship, but one with a high comfort level. There is loyalty and good communication between them. Over time they can forge a lasting friendship but they need time to build a strong and stable relationship. It cannot happen instantly. Communication between them must steadily increase.

Ox appreciates the accommodating nature of Dog and finds life with this sign embracing and easy. Their relationship is rarely strenuous because Dog is amiable and loyal. But Ox must curb its tendency to take Dog for granted, because when least expected, Dog might just bark back. Most times however, Dog will almost always take the line of least resistance and go along with what Ox wants. In 2011, both Dog and Ox have low energy levels, but Dog has a powerful ally in the year's dominant Rabbit energy being its secret friend, so Ox would benefit from getting its Dog partner completely on its side.

The problem in this union is that Dog might listen to other opinions and resent Ox's seeming indifference. Outsiders can cast evil eyes on this relationship, sending bad vibes their way and causing a certain amount of tension to manifest between them. Indeed, when two people seem to have success come so easily, any jealousy generated can take on cosmic strength that is harmful, so this couple must communicate more with each other. They also benefit from having protective amulets in their space. This guards against outsiders spoiling what you have together.

For this pair to take fullest advantage of the year, they should listen more to one another and less to others. They can also be a little more demonstrative and vocal in their high personal regard of each other. Nothing works better than a few carefully chosen words of tenderness to bring a strained relationship back on track.

DOG WITH TIGER
Amazing pair & very auspicious too

The year 2011 is a great year for these two allies of the Zodiac. This is when good things come equally big and as powerful to both signs of the Tiger and the Dog; and the great news is that you will both stay true to one another. Tiger and Dog continue to be good for each other and also continue to need each other.

The Tiger's affections for the Dog arises as much from Dog's dependability as a soulmate as from Dog's steadfastness and loyalty. These sentiments are likewise reciprocated by Dog, so this is a couple who can work in tandem to manifest the excellent indications in their horoscope and respective feng shui chart locations. Their allegiance to one another brings excellent results in what looks to be a really excellent year for both.

The Tiger and Dog are lucky this year. Tiger enjoys the luck of victory, while Dog feels the auspicious luck of the number 8 flying into its location. True, Dog continues to have a low level indication for its life force and inner essence, but the power of 8 more than makes up for this.

Those married to one another will find that simply standing together in 2011 will bring them good fortune.

Comrades Climb High ♥♥♥♥

The two signs' numbers in the feng shui chart enjoy what we refer to as the white numbers combination – these are the numbers 1 and 8 which indicate that together, the strength of the white numbers get doubled. It is possible that this pair can develop and grow something truly meaningful between them.

Tiger and Dog are usually great for each other irrespective of what the year brings. They bring out the best in each other and there is genuine love and understanding flowing between them. There are also no competitive issues or pressures that can be so strong as to burst their happiness bubble.

> They make friends easily and can work well in business together; indeed, it is likely that they start out as work colleagues becoming lifelong partners.

The good news for this well matched pair then is that 2011 promises to be excellent for them to build something together. They can move ahead with confidence, reach for the skies and climb as high as they want to. Indeed, having each other to share the climb and the high of victories is what will make their lives meaningful. This is the essence of happiness, something worth pursuing.

DOG WITH RABBIT
Leaning on Dog's kindness

The Rabbit who is in love with a Dog sign is lucky indeed, because here you have someone who is not just going through a relatively strong year and is thus able to support and nurture you, but this is also a person capable of great kindness. Dog is famous for being a good friend to anyone close to them, and because the Rabbit is your secret friend, you are likely to be of great help. Rabbit benefits more than any other sign in a relationship with the Dog.

But Rabbit already instinctively knows this as it tends to gravitate to Dog without much prompting. In a year when Rabbit needs real and true friends, they will not trust anyone too readily; the lovely aura of Dog's energy however will be like a magnet for them. Dog enjoys a year when its energy is radiant and glowing. This is a sign that will have some ups and downs in its luck quota for the year but all this pales into insignificance as Dog enjoys the mighty power of 8. This is such a strong indication that in many ways, this could even turn out to be a spectacular year for Dog.

Rabbit on the other hand must endure the *wu wang* or five yellow, so in terms of chi energy, there is something of a mismatch here. but because there are binding ties caused by the horoscope, far from being turned off Rabbit, Dog finds being needed both satisfying and fulfilling.

> If this pair are already married, Dog's energy should carry them through the year, helping Rabbit to survive its afflictions. Between them is genuine trust and understanding. They aspire to the same things in life and are in tune with each other's moods, attitudes and preferences. Theirs is potentially a very happy marriage as they can be good friends as well as good lovers.

The setback here for this pair is that in 2011, both Rabbit and Dog are rather lacking in energy; they must work at galvanising each other, giving strength to each other and building one another's confidence.

The good thing about the Rabbit and Dog pairing is that irrespective of their luck, this does not affect the quality of their relationship and they are as loving during good or bad times. Their genuine affection for each other is usually strong enough to ride through obstacles and setbacks.

DOG WITH DRAGON
Natural enemies find common ground

It is a well-publicised fact that anyone born in the year of the Dog will find it hard to bond well with those born in the year of the Dragon; indeed, enemies of the Zodiac tend to be rather ferocious with one another most of the time, although Dog tends to play down the enmity. But in 2011 the Dragon and Dog unexpectedly find common ground, with the Dragon being less vocal or rude to the Dog.

In the year of the Rabbit, these Yang Earth animal signs will find their differences becoming unimportant - with the Rabbit year bonding them powerfully together. The Rabbit year's energies find favor with the benevolent Dog, and also with its seasonal friend the Dragon. Hence in the year of the Rabbit, Dragon and Dog set aside their differences and start to bond well. This benefits Dog more than it does Dragon, because for Dragon, getting into a love relationship with Dog is like sleeping with the enemy. It is actually quite rare for these two signs to live harmoniously together and should they be married, it is unlikely to be a smooth or compatible relationship.

These two signs aspire to different goals in life, and although both may be equally ambitious, they differ very much in their attitudes and manner of making it in the world. The Dog personality is almost always a lot more low key than that of the Dragon. Also in matters of romance and love, Dragon is more likely to wear its heart on its sleeve than Dog. One lacks the subtlety of the other.

Happily however, 2011 is a good time for them to bury their differences and enjoy the best of each other. And indeed there is a gold mine of good intentions on both sides. Surprisingly, Dragon will automatically get drawn to Dog's success aura while Dog responds positively to Dragon's heavenly demeanor. Indeed, Dragon is less aggressive this year than it usually is.

The **59 year old Water Dragon** is very agreeable indeed as will be the other Dragons although less so; but the Dog personality is extremely pleasant in 2011.

> For them, the year is delightful and filled with rosy vibrations and even the enemy exudes good vibes for them. For these natural enemies of the Zodiac, the year will be both pleasurable and enjoyable; and it makes good common sense to make as much as you can from this period.

DOG WITH SNAKE
Attraction is mutual and full of sparks

In the year 2011, Dog enjoys the company of Snake. Their personalities are in sync this year as both will glow in the limelight fuelled along by a continuous momentum of good times and even better vibrations. This is not a pair that gets naturally drawn to each other, but in 2011, their strong auras glow with a brightness that acts like a natural antenna for one another. So attraction between them is mutual, generating lots of sparks and pulling them together.

In 2011, both Dog and Snake possess some powerful energy brought by the feng shui winds of the year. As a couple, you can keep up with each other and you will find pleasure in doing the same things. It is not at all like the previous year, so if you are meeting one another for the first time, it is sure to be a blast!

Traditionally, Dog and Snake do not have much that draws them together. You are not astrologically linked in any way and there is little to bond you to the Snake personality. So the relationship will find its own comfort zone, and this is likely to be at a relatively shallow level. This should not in any way put you off each other and happily does not do so in 2011. Both of you are perfectly acceptable of the fact that it is not

Excellent Compatibility ♥♥♥

really necessary to operate at such deep levels. For both of you, the year 2011 can be as superficial as anything and you will still enjoy all the goodies that come to you both. If finding one another is the highlight of the year, you are practical enough to simply sit back and enjoy.

> In 2011, Dog is strengthened by the power of 8. Success luck is at an all-time high and relationship luck is also strong. Snake resonates with Dog's optimistic and positive attitude this year and finds the Dog personality very attractive.

If Snake and Dog are married, both experience a renewed sense of discovery. Snake responds to the promise of new excitement offered by an empowered Dog, so there is a chance for the year to be a lot more pleasant than last year.

The good thing about these two signs is their practical and down-to-earth attitude towards life and relationships. Whatever bad vibes may have been created before get swept away, as these are two people who can shrug off past hurts and look ahead instead. This is the key to their happiness through the year.

DOG WITH HORSE
Allies bite off more than they can chew

Who can blame the Horse and Dog who are in a relationship together from becoming over-confident or excessively ambitious in 2011? This is a year when these allies of the Zodiac are riding high, buoyed by wonderful feng shui winds for Dog that rub off on Horse, causing sparks to fly and a special kind of excitement to get generated.

> Dog and Horse are part of an alliance of faithful allies with the Tiger, so between them is a special affinity that engenders trust and great fidelity. They are not just lovers then, but also good friends, and in 2011, the great vitality of Horse resonates brilliantly with Dog's aura. Why? Because Dog is embraced by the power of 8; the super abundant star number which has flown to Dog's location, bringing with it the promise of prosperity and great abundance.

The positive signs in the charts for these two animals augur very well for their already close relationship, and although Dog's personalised energy may be weaker than that of Horse, it is more than made up for by the power of 8. What is great is that Horse's super duper energy is somewhat tempered by the *Star of Reducing*

Over-ambitious ♥♥♥♥

Energy that it is sitting on. This makes Horse calmer and more tolerant, which of course adds to the synergy between this set of allies.

The energy of this pair is thus very favorable, with each bringing out the best in the other. This defines their compatibility, making it easy for them to live amiably together and also to work towards achieving a shared goal. The good news is that Horse and Dog are also very similar in their values, in their thought processes and in what is really important for them both.

What one does is sure to resonate well with the other. They have a great comfort zone between them, and in 2011 have quite a lot to look forward to. The conflicting energies of the year will not shake their idyll and in fact could bring them closer than ever together.

They just need to be less demanding of themselves so there is not too much pressure on the Horse especially. It is also advisable to perhaps scale back on their aspirations for the year 2011, as doing so is sure to be an insurance from being disappointed.

DOG WITH SHEEP
Finding companionship and love in 2011

Dog is both attractive and extremely willing in 2011 and Sheep has love in its viewfinder, so this is a year when notions of romance between this pair can take root, grow and blossom. As with last year, sparks are sure to ignite between this pair, except that in 2011, the fires of love tend to burn stronger. And it is the kind that can lead to something more permanent too.

The Dog and Sheep are surprisingly very compatible this year, finding an easy familiarity and a natural leaning towards each other. These are two of the Zodiac's more gentle and caring signs; they are also loyal and nurturing towards those they love. For them, love grows slowly but surely, and once committed, they tend to be faithful and trusting. This pair is thus happy to gravitate towards each other, and then end up having eyes only for each other. It is a very happy situation, one that is also precious and not to be taken for granted.

Relationships like this can be hard to find and develop, and for both, the year helps you along. Dog especially is enjoying the support of the great power of 8 which brings good vibes - relationships tend to proceed smoothly for you this year and with Sheep being so

Commitment ♥ ♥ ♥ ♥ ♥

grounded and practical in 2011, all the signs look very promising indeed.

> Those of you involved in a relationship as an eager Sheep or a willing Dog would do well to cherish the love you have for one another. This is a great year to create a commitment towards one another.

The Dog and Sheep are not stubborn people and are rarely quick to anger. They are easy going and sensitive, so this can be a very nice and stable bond that can stand the test of time. But for those already married to one another however, do not expect that what you need is grand passion. Yours is a steady, stable and solid kind of togetherness and not the loud intense kind of excitement. You are two people who prefer unwavering loyalty to flamboyant fervor.

So in both a love or work relationship, this couple pairs well. But if you are hoping to have an affair of the heart or be engaging in some kind of illicit relationship, it is doomed from the start, because you are simply not the kind of people who are made that way. For both of you, love must mean commitment, not just a passionate fling you can walk away from.

DOG WITH MONKEY
In 2011 cosmic sparks fly between this pair

In 2011, Dog and Monkey find many reasons to celebrate, with the ebullient Dog taking the lead. Somehow, Dog is feeling confident and strong and 2011 could well become a significant year for this pair. The general feel-good aura of Dog permeates this relationship quite noticeably. In the Monkey and Dog couple, it is usually Monkey who takes the lead, calling the shots and being the dominant partner; but in 2011, we see a gentle reversal of roles, spawned as much by the feng shui winds of the year as by the way the constellation seems to be enhancing Dog's cosmic ambience.

> Monkey is smitten by Dog's air of great auric strength, and strongly fuelled by the year's favorable indications, Dog could even be in something of a combative mode. Anyone coming close to Dog will do better being friends than adversaries, and Monkey is happy to sail along with the way the winds blow.

This is a couple who are at their best during the season of Fall, when the harvest is done and all that's left is to prepare for the coming new year. Autumn is also a time when the season is getting colder, when its time to think of slowing down and to allow for rest and recreation. This is also a time of the year when it is advisable to have harmony in the home, for it is this harmony that enhances the luck for the rest of the year which then carries through to the new year. This is the advantage of the Monkey/Dog pairing - that they instinctively know this, so that with Dog enjoying such superlative good energy from the feng shui chart, Monkey is clever enough to go along for the ride...

In 2010, Dog is blessed by the power of 8 and although in terms of its element interaction with the year's elements it shows Dog is weak, nevertheless the feng shui winds of the year are very favorable. This helps Dog overcome a variety of small setbacks.

Monkey meanwhile is feeling romantic, prepared to sit back and enjoy a new love interest or have its love life seriously jazzed up. The horoscope element charts indicate Monkey being stronger than Dog. But Dog has the power of 8 and also enjoys the *Star of Small Auspicious*. Monkey is not helped by anything lucky coming from the 24 mountain constellation, so it seems really good all round for Monkey to simply ride on the back of Dog's good vibrations, enjoying the sparks generated.

DOG WITH ROOSTER
A hollow feeling generates distance

Dog has a seasonal Zodiac connection with Rooster that makes them extra compatible during the months of Autumn. Together with the Monkey, this pair create the combination that enhances their season of Fall, when the world is attuned to harvesting. Generally also, Dog gets along well with anyone born in the year of the Rooster, and in certain circumstances, can even forge a strong and powerful alliance.

This is a pairing that has great potential for happiness as they are supportive and caring of each other, but the divide between them in 2011 might create a distance that eventually causes their relationship to degenerate into awkward silences and uneasy interactions. Why is this? Mainly because Dog is riding high and Rooster is too distracted to compliment or rejoice. It is this mismatching of the year's largesse that might cause misunderstandings to upset this relationship.

Being in one another's company somehow causes a hollow kind of feeling inside them, as a result of which both sides turn away, tending to their own pursuits. Dog feels hassled by lack of time and Rooster is feeling misunderstood and inadequate and could even descend into a spiral of unfamiliar self pity. There are

Awkward & Uneasy ♥♥♥

times this year when it can get rather depressing for them both.

> The problem will be that Dog can get so carried away by all the new people coming into its life engaging its attention that they succumb to pleading lack of time. Done too often causes Rooster to turn away.

This is a year when Dog knows that Rooster needs to address some problems. Luckily, Rooster is feeling strong, although this makes for a lethal combination. Needing help, Rooster will be too proud to ask, thus sowing the seeds of discontent that can fester within the relationship with Dog. It is likely that misunderstandings will arise due to a clash of bruised egos, which cause this normally unflappable pair to get annoyed and maybe just give up on the relationship.

Dog enjoys a potentially great year but is weak and therefore easily influenced. This is not good for its relationship with Rooster. Rooster's energ are high and luck not so good, while Dog's energy is weak but luck fantastic. So if Rooster can subdue its underlying jealousy and rejoice with Dog's good fortune, then the year will bring good things for them both.

DOG WITH DOG
Bringing out best & worst in one another

Two Dogs in a relationship can make a cosy, warm love fest or it can be can bring out the aggressive nature in one another. Much depends on their individual personality traits and there can be so many variations as to what kind of Dog person you are that the extremes of your attitudes get activated this year. So you will either bring out the best or the worst in one another. But no matter how you love or bash it out through the year, it is certain that 2011 will turn out fine for you both. It is an excellent time when good feng shui winds bring good news and better developments. In a Rabbit year, your secret friend, the chi energy of the cosmic space around you is favorable. You also benefit from the abundance-bringing power 8. Astrologically, the year pans out really well indeed.

The feng shui energies this year are supportive and encouraging. In terms of work and professional pursuits, there is little that can go wrong. So Dog people will be very confident and receptive this year. In your relationships however, there could be a tendency towards becoming more aggressive than usual, and this might make you aggravated and impatient. When and if you feel your temper rising, it is a good idea to just walk away, cool down, then come back and make up. Dog people do not hold grudges. Nor do they stay angry for long, so in a pairing between two Dogs, there is rarely danger of quarrels getting out of hand.

Dogs are naturally gentle and basically kind, having a forgiving nature. So in 2011, with the year's energies being so favorable, the influence of the yearly conflict star brought by the constellation of the 24 mountains should not cause too many problems. This is a star that is easy to keep in check. If one word sums up the best attitude to have this year, it is to stay super cool.

> When two Dogs live together, they sink into a comfort level, easily respecting their own space and getting their lives organised in an efficient way. These are people who are easy to live with, and with 2011 being such a good year there will also be few negatives to cause trouble in their life.

The only thing a pair of Dogs have to take note of are their element energy levels. Their chi essence and life force are weak and so health considerations take on a significance. But with the 8 star, illness is unlikely to be too big a problem. The Dog continues to enjoy the good vibrations felt last year and 2011 will see them successfully building on whatever was started last year.

DOG WITH BOAR
An easy going relationship in 2011

The Dog and Boar continue their amiable relationship of the previous year and whatever happiness or success they may have achieved with one another continues to grow and flourish. Theirs is an easy-going relationship and this more than anything keeps them satisfied and tolerant. In any case, the year 2011 brings so much good stuff that they will find time will fly by. We can thus say that it will be excellent all the way for this pair.

The feng shui chart of the year reveals that these two signs share the auspicious power number of 8 which brings the luck of wealth and abundance as well as much happiness too. The 8 is a very auspicious number as it reinforces the energy of the current period suggesting that whatever gets started or developed this year will be successful. This augurs well for the Dog, enabling it to also enjoy a series of success developments. Those in politics or some kind of elective position will not only enjoy success this year but with Boar by its side, Dog will have not only a successful year but a happy one as well.

Dog has an easy relationship with Boar that is not in any way marred by petty insensitivities or misunderstandings. Theirs is a mature approach, so there is a wonderful absence of childish tantrums and mind games. Both sides appreciate the generally untroubled and unruffled way they approach the business of living, so philosophically, this is a good match. There is sincerity and genuine affection flowing between them, so it is not difficult for them to create their own space yet with room left over for the other.

> Those who have just met will enjoy the year and find happiness in each other, while those of you who are already in a relationship should find yourselves scaling greater heights and also going deeper with each other. It is excellent all the way.

An effective way to build on the good fortune of the year and to cement your strong bonds with one another is to create something auspicious in the Northwest of your home or garden such as planting an auspicious fruit tree (e.g. the pomegranate plant is very suitable) or decorating the Northwest wall of your home with something auspicious such as a family photograph with the both of you (and your children if any) smiling broadly.

Dog's Monthly Horoscope 2011

Good Timing of Month Stars Helps Dog Benefit from the Year

The Dog person enjoys an excellent year when the feng shui chart brings the auspicious number 8 into its location. This indicates that you can achieve much success this year, and wealth luck especially looks very good. Although the 24 mountains constellation stars are not so promising, with the Star of Yearly Conflict flying into your location, you do have the Star of Small Auspicious coming from the direction of the Boar. This suggests that Boar friends and associates will be especially lucky for you this year, particularly in terms of small successes but ones that bring much happiness and personal joy. Your Life Force and Chi Strength this year however are not so robust, so it is a good idea to carry mantra protection as a shield against falling victim to spirit harm.

1ST MONTH
February 4th - March 5th 2011

EXCELLENT INDICATIONS BRING GOOD VIBES

The year starts off quite fabulously for the Dog person with the completion star of 9 joining the wealth star of 8, thereby strengthening it as well as lending to the year a most auspicious start. It is believed that when you strike off the year on a good note, it sets the tone for the rest of the year, so it is really a good idea to make the most of this month by using every last ounce of your energy to seize the opportunities that come your way. You will be bursting with creativity and enthusiasm, so getting in the swing of life in the fast lane should be easy for you. Put your good ideas into motion and get things going. You're laying the groundwork for the next 12 months; don't let this month go to waste or you could well "miss the boat".

WORK & CAREER - *Flying High*

Career luck is flying high for the Dog. This is a month when you can use your talents to impress the people who matter. Don't be afraid to stick out like a sore thumb. Although your job may have required protocol in the past, now is the time to trust your instincts to let your talents come forth. Banish your fear of treading on the toes of jealous, disgruntled colleagues. You're excellent with your people skills and can easily build rapport, so instead of dodging the feelings of competitive co-workers, get to work at winning over their confidence and build up your army of allies.

BUSINESS - *Networking Brings Benefits*
There's plenty of good fortune in store for Dog people in business this month. Your luck is on an upward trend so this is a good time to take a higher profile and to get yourself noticed. Advertising, marketing and promotional activities go well for you this month, and you can gain a lot of good publicity if you make the effort. You won't even have to spend too much. You can continue to be budget conscious, but don't be overly miserly when it comes to spending to promote yourself or your product. Aggressive networking takes you a long way and you have the energy to do it. Besides, you quite enjoy this aspect of your work, so putting more effort into this won't just improve your business prospects, you'll be having the time of your life.

LOVE & RELATIONSHIPS - *Romance Rules*
Romance rule the month and there's much to make your heart go a-flutter. There are numerous opportunities to forget everything else and just follow your heart. You can afford to do that if you're young

and without a care in the world, but for those of you with other responsibilities in life, you may need to make a conscious effort not to neglect them. This is a deceptive month because you're riding a horoscope chart that's filled with lucky stars. Seize the moment and be as passionate as you want, but don't do anything that will leave room for regret later on.

Dogs aiming to settle down may find this something difficult to do this month. Those of you already married will find it even harder to stay faithful. Don't let yourself be tempted by amorous influences outside your marriage. You are by nature a loyal partner, and mistakes made in a moment of weakness will be far more damaging to the Dog person than to anything else. Don't let yourself become weak on this front, or it will be you who ultimately suffers.

EDUCATION – *Turbo-charged*
The student Dog benefits just as much from the turbo-charged energies of the month as your older Dog counterparts. You shine in your academic career and also do well in extracurricular activities. There are many victories awaiting you, so don't hesitate to take on a challenge. If you are a competitive person, this is a good month to pursue competitive ventures, whether in music, sport or scholarship hunting.

2ND MONTH
March 6th - April 4th 2011

GOOD FORTUNE DOUBLES

You enjoy superb luck this month, one which brings success and triumph in double doses. You have luck coming at you from all directions, so much you won't know what to do with it! But luck helps those who help themselves. Luck can only give you better odds than the next person, but ultimately it is up to you. When your luck is so good, your responsibility to yourself is to make the most of it. This is a month to go out there and show the world what you're made of. By all means take some risks, but don't be foolhardy. While you enjoy a multitude of auspicious indications in your feng shui chart, your life force is on the low end of the scale, so make sure you carry adequate protection to ensure you don't succumb to the bad intentions of those with the evil eye. It is a good idea to carry the **anti-evil-eye amulet** this month.

WORK & CAREER – *Making Friends*

Working life goes well for the Dog. You're likely to finally have a clear idea of where you see your career going, and those of you who have hopped jobs in the past may finally be happy where you are. You pick up knowledge at an amazing speed this month, so make it a point to learn as much as you can. And don't think you can only learn from those earning big salaries. Your own peers have a lot to teach you. Don't make your co-workers your rivals; instead, get them on your side and work together to move up the career ladder. You have the ability to build some lifelong friendships this month.

BUSINESS - *New Ways of Doing Things*

Business luck looks very promising this month. This is a good time to keep a look out for new potential areas of growth. Sales will be up and financially you are secure. This month sees you relaxing when it comes to money issues, allowing you to look forward with plans for growth and expansion. If you are heading your company operationally, many new ways of doing things will dawn on you. Some of these ideas will come out of the blue; others will be picked up in the course of your networking. You are astute when it comes to picking up gems of information that prove useful. An excellent month indeed, when direction from you benefits the business significantly.

> Carry the anti-evil-eye amulet to avoid attracting the attention of people who may become jealous of you.

LOVE & RELATIONSHIPS – *In Control*

You're in control when it comes to the dating game, so it's really a matter of who you like best. If you stay single through the month, it'll only be because no one measured up to your high standards. Happiness is doubled when you can share it with someone special, so if you really can't find your true love, perhaps you should consider rethinking your standards. Those of you who are married will probably be more content than your single Dog counterparts. There is a new ease in your marriage, and loving vibes flow easily between you and your spouse. If you're not getting along the way you would like, perhaps it's time to make more time for your partner.

EDUCATION – *Open Your Mind*

Things go well for the young Dog this month. You are full of confidence and poise. Doing well in your class assignments comes easily for you, and you make astute and meaningful contributions to class discussion. Your social life becomes more interesting and enjoyable, with some new friends entering the picture. Be open to learning from new people this month; there is a lot to learn and if you open your mind, you stand to benefit a great deal.

3RD MONTH
April 5th - May 5th 2011

FEELING OF BEING DOUBLE CROSSED

Your luck dips this month. You might be feeling ill at ease with yourself, and see the actions of others somewhat as little betrayals. It is easy to rile you with the violent star making an appearance. The number 7 also brings threat of robbery and being cheated, so you may not be all wrong when you find yourself more mistrustful or suspicious of others. Be more alert this month. Carry or wear protection in the form of mantra jewellery or a mantra bag hanging. Lady Dogs should beware when out and about late at night. In business, avoid taking risks or entering into new contracts and agreements this month. Keep a watchful eye on your finances. Those of you working your way up the career ladder may have to deal with some petty office politics this month.

WORK & CAREER - *Office Politics*

Office politics may rear its ugly head this month. This may cause you undue stress. Your best bet is to keep a low profile and avoid getting sucked into the snake pit of corporate backstabbing. Avoid taking sides, bad-mouthing or giving your opinions on too many things. You may end up saying the wrong thing and this will only put you in a bad light. It is much better to get on with your work, even if it means suffering some small indignities. Lashing out in anger and frustration will lead to bad news this month. Just make sure you have a **Rooster figurine** on your desk to keep you on the sidelines and to protect yourself from becoming a victim.

BUSINESS – *Avoid Socializing Too Much*
This is not a good month to invest. Maintain the status quo. Avoid socializing too much, for you may find you have the knack of getting into difficult conversational situations. Steer clear of too many corporate cocktails and the networking circuit. There are times when you are the master of dinner party conversation, but this month you don't enjoy that advantage. If you're looking to socialize this month, keep it strictly light-hearted, with family and friends you trust. Avoid important meetings with outsiders if you can; if you can't reschedule meetings, keep the conversation light and innocuous.

LOVE & RELATIONSHIPS – *Keep Things Light*
Not a great month when it comes to your love life. Avoid making any big moves this month even if

you know what you want to say. If there's someone special you have your eye on, continue the pursuit but leave the serious stuff till next month. It is best to concentrate on other areas of your life right now than to be madly doing the social scene. If you are already in a steady relationship, you may find this a frustrating month with uncharacteristic fights between yourself and your partner. You may have to learn to give in more. But whatever you do, don't give a third party outsider the chance to intrude and interfere with your relationship.

EDUCATION – *Working Under Pressure*
Things may not go as well as they have for the last two months, but you overcome difficulties in your studies easily if you make yourself to take charge. Don't give up on anything or lose hope. You may have to work harder to achieve the same grades and results right now, but this difficult time will pass. Those of you who work well under pressure could find this month quite rewarding.

FRIENDSHIPS – *Strained*
Your relationships with friends could get a little strained this month. You could feel let down by someone you considered a close friend. Their intention may not be bad, so give them the benefit of the doubt.

4TH MONTH
May 6th - June 5th 2011

GREAT MONTH WITH POWERFUL TOP LEVEL SUPPORT

Your luck improves manifold and you enjoy blessings from heaven this month. Mentor luck in particular gets enhanced so you could see yourself getting backed by someone at the top. A fabulous month for ambitious Dog people looking to make it in the corporate world. There are many good opportunities that come your way, and if you can maintain the support of the people who matter, you're well on your way to making the most of these opportunities. When something come along, be ready to rise to the occasion. You may be prodded out of your comfort zone a little bit this month, but once you start enjoying the taste of success, it becomes addictive. Get yourself caught into this upward spiral and you could be setting yourself up for wonderful things to come.

WORK & CAREER - *Be Proactive*

Your potential knows no bounds this month, so it is a time to move resolutely forward and go after what you want. If you have been sitting idle waiting for that promotion, perhaps it is time to stop waiting and start doing something about it. Don't wait for tasks to be set for you. Be proactive and show your superiors you can be depended on. Ask for more work if you can handle it, or better yet, suggest what you can do to contribute more. It will be appreciated and well rewarded. Boost the luck of allies and supporters by carrying your **horoscope friends and allies** with you as a personal amulet.

BUSINESS - Stay Well Informed

Dealings in business go very well for you this month as you have much good fortune on your side. Engage in discussions, negotiations and dialogue with business associates. The outcome will turn out in your favor nearly every time. Be sure to use your Kua formula whenever you find yourself in an important discussion. If you keep to this rule, you won't fall short of your potential this month.

Use the advice of friends and mentor figures in the know. Keep your ears to the ground so you are well informed about market trends. It is important to keep abreast of the news or you may miss something. Though opportunities will be thrust your way this month, the best way to gain from them is to be up to date and in the know.

LOVE & RELATIONSHIPS – *Pleasurable*

This is a fabulous month for Dogs to get married, conceive a child or begin new relationships. Love blossoms in all forms in your life and you are both materially and spiritually fulfilled. This is one of those magic months when you find both your professional and personal life on top form. Make the most of this happy time and learn to enjoy yourself! Your happiness will rub off on all those around you, which in turn will bring you even more joy. Those of you who are still single could well find your potential mate this month. To speed things up in the love process, wear the double happiness symbol as jewellery or carry it as a symbol in your wallet.

EDUCATION – *Mentor Luck*

Your mentor luck is strong this month. This indicates you can benefit from having someone to look up to, confide in and emulate. It is important to choose your mentor well, and in most cases, your parents will make good candidates. However, having a mentor closer to your student life such as a teacher or an older student will help you gain ground when it comes to your academic ambitions.

5TH MONTH
June 6th - July 6th 2011

MINOR SETBACKS AFFECT YOUR CONFIDENCE

The misfortune star makes an appearance this month, so it is better to err on the side of caution. The best way to battle the inauspicious stars in your chart is by keeping a low profile and resisting the urge to stray from the well-trodden path. Avoid making hurried decisions. Anything done in haste this month is likely to have unfortunate results. You may come up against frustrating obstacles or hit small bouts of misfortune. Don't let them get you down. Stay tenacious and the difficulties will pass as quickly as they start. This is a month when good friends are important. You need to know who to trust and who will do you in at the first opportunity. Boost your ally luck by displaying your allies and secret friend in the Northwest corner of your home or office.

WORK & CAREER - *Temporary Hiccups*

Things may not be going as well as they have done in the past few months. This is a temporary hiccup in the grater scheme of things. The monthly five yellow can cause a lot of havoc, but if you know how to suppress it, you can get through the month unscathed. Carry or wear the five element pagoda. Get the pagoda with the tree of life, as this has the power to transform this afflictive star into a lucky one, allowing you to turn setbacks into opportunities. Things may not be what they seem. Maintain confidence in yourself and in your good fortune this year. Once the month passes, you start to see that some of what you termed bad luck at the time happened for a reason.

BUSINESS – Be Cautious

While your overall business luck is good this year, you need to take caution this month. Keep your eyes and ears open to changes in mood and scenery. Don't follow your instincts alone when making decisions. Try to be as informed as you can so you can make carefully thought out strategic decisions.

You may have a lot on your mind, but this is not the time to speak out, especially if you have something radical to propose. Keeping the status quo is the best way to maintain your luck through this patchy month. This is a good time to plan a holiday and take a break from work for a while. It is not a bad month for non-financial pursuits. Focus on the spiritual rather than the material this month.

LOVE & RELATIONSHIPS - *Learn to Listen*

Although you probably have too much on your mind to worry about your love life right now, this is one of those times when you could really do with some support from someone who cares. It is a better time for relationships already well established than for new ones. Those of you who are married will draw a lot of support from your spouse this month. Interacting in a light-hearted way with someone else will take your mind off other worries in your life, so putting some attention to matters of the heart may not be such a bad thing. However, for those pursuing a new love interest, your date may find you somewhat self centered in your conversation. Remember to listen as well as talk, if you want your budding relationship to have a chance.

HEALTH & SAFETY - *Look After Yourself*

You are at risk of careless accidents around the house this month, so avoid construction, renovation and handy work. You may meet with some personal misfortunes because of the malevolent stars in your chart. Make sure you have a **Pi Yao** in your home this month, and place a **five-element pagoda with tree of life** in the NW for this month. This will help protect you and your family against bad luck.

6TH MONTH
July 7th - Aug 7th 2011

ROMANTIC ATTRACTION ENGAGES YOUR EMOTIONS

Your luck perks up, especially when it comes to socializing, romancing and developing friendships. You become more upbeat and more fun to be around. Expect some good news to come your way soon. Even if the news is not directly related to you, getting involved in someone else's happiness will have a very positive effect on you indeed. You have much creative energy in you and if you can apply this to your work, you can do superbly well this month. Writers, scholars, students and anyone with an inclination towards the literary will flourish this month. A great month to fall in love and be swept off your feet! The only thing to watch out for this month is the danger of infidelity. There will be a lot of people flocking to you vying for your attention, but there may be some whose motives are not altogether savory. Stay sensible and don't let yourself make a mistake that could cause you much strife in your marriage and personal life. It is a good idea to wear the **Rooster with Amethyst and Fan** if you are happily married.

WORK & CAREER - *New Possibilities*

Others find you a delight to work with this month. You handle your relationships extremely well, knowing just how to set the tone, both with your co-workers as well as your boss. This is a month when opportunities come with new people who appear on the scene. Pay close attention to the people around you. You may be offered a huge opportunity and not even see it if you don't open your mind to new possibilities. Stop yourself from being overly cynical about new ideas. If something excites you, don't let the grounded side of your personality hold you back. This is a month when anything can happen. Let your dreams take wing and fly with them.

BUSINESS - *Lots of Options*

There are many avenues to go down and different directions to take this month. You are facing a minefield of good ideas. If you've been operating as a one-man show, this is a good time to start allocating tasks. Effective delegation will get you much further than trying to do everything yourself. Learn to trust your staff and subordinates. You may have been molly-coddling them in the past, but if you throw them in the deep end, they will swim. Taking on a mentoring role this month will do much for productivity in your company. It is sometimes as much in the mind as it is in the level of skill available.

LOVE & RELATIONSHIPS – *Stay in Control*

You're in for quite a ride this month when it comes to passion and romance. You're the object of many people's affections and could even find yourself caught in the middle of a love triangle. Don't play with fire when it comes to love. There are many temptations that come your way, and there is also danger of falling under bad influence. Stay in control of your emotions, no matter how hard it may seem. You can be just as happy this way. Don't let your head get turned by the promise of excitement and illicit romance. You're a homebody at heart and while playing with fire could be tempting at first, you'll soon regret the aftermath.

EDUCATION – *Try Your Hand at New Things*

This is a wonderful month for the student Dog. Academically you are doing great, leaving you enough time in a day to also nurture the other areas of your life. This is a month when pursuing sport, music, art and other extracurricular activities brings much satisfaction. And when you discover what you're good at, you become even more motivated to do well at it. A good time to try new things and to take on new hobbies and activities.

7TH MONTH
Aug 8th - Sept 7th 2011

HOSTILITY LEADS TO INTOLERANCE

There is both good and bad luck indicated in your horoscope charts this month. The bad luck comes in the form of arguments, quarrels and even lawsuits. You could find yourself more short-tempered than usual. The people around you may irk you more. They too may appear more argumentative. Watch your words before you speak. Saying the wrong thing to the wrong person could lose you your big chance of success. Be particularly careful in your professional life not to offend the wrong people. If you have any harsh words, hold back and keep them to yourself. Don't let yourself indulge in gossip as it will definitely backfire this month. The good news is that there is a pot of gold at the end of the rainbow with the quarrelsome star forming a Ho Tu combination with the annual star, but the road to that gold is littered with potholes in the form of your own short temper.

WORK & CAREER - *Challenging*

Getting along with your colleagues may prove something of a challenge this month. There may be one or two of them who could really rub you up the wrong way, but keeping your cool and keeping them on your side is your best bet this month. Don't get yourself in a situation where you develop a combative relationship with your co-workers. Your luck when it comes to face-offs and challenges is down this month, and in any fight, you will lose. Work at maintaining a cordial relationship with those you work with. You could find yourself getting worked up over small things, but once your rivals work this out, they know your weakness and will get you every time.

BUSINESS - *Fierce Competition*

There is indication of much fiercer competition this month than you are accustomed to. Armed with the knowledge that you have good fortune luck this month, you can be confident when making your moves, but resist fraternizing with the enemy lest you let on too much or lose your cool in conversation. If you have regular contact with your business associates, carry a **Peace amulet** to help keep your energies calm and to protect you against saying the wrong thing.

Carry the Peace amulet to suppress the quarrelsome vibes that plague you this month.

LOVE & RELATIONSHIPS – *Mood Swings*

This month romance fizzles out of your life a little, due mostly to your quarrelsome mood. Your partner may be done putting up with your mood swings and could be needing some space. The biggest problem right now is not knowing what you want. You can't seem to get along with other people but yet you want them around. You need someone to listen, but you're unwilling to listen back. Work harder at being a good companion if you want good companionship back. And if you're looking for romance, you're going to have to do a lot to earn it this month!

EDUCATION – *Tough Going*

Things may be a little tough this month because of the quarrelsome energies that surround you. Try not to get too worked up over issues. If you disagree with others on what you've got planned for yourself, take a long hard look at why you want to do things your way. When you analyze it that way, your point of view may not seem so good after all. Your judgment is a little off, so outside opinions will go far in helping you make the right decisions this month.

8TH MONTH
Sept 8th - Oct 7th 2011

HEALTH AILMENTS CAN GET SERIOUS

The illness star flies into your sector this month, bringing threats to your health. If you feel something is not right with you, it is probably better to get checked out. Don't soldier on despite feeling doggedly ill or minor ailments could turn more serious. Protect against health problems with a **Wu Lou** by your bedside. You can also wear the **longevity** symbol. Try to keep sensible hours when it comes to your sleep patterns. It may be tempting to work through the night if there are tight deadlines to meet, but this could just end up slowing you down. When exhaustion takes over, you'll find yourself making careless mistakes, some of which could have some dire consequences. It is a much better idea to try and schedule your time better.

Display a pair of Wu Lou by your bedside to counter the illness energies of the month.

WORK & CAREER - *Don't Take On Too Much*

You may find yourself quite easily distracted this month and this could affect the quality of your work. Disturbed sleep patterns will also make it more difficult to be productive during the day. Try herbal remedies to improve your concentration level, or use a natural crystal point to sharpen your mind and to increase your ability to focus. You need to try harder this month simply because you tend to be more careless. In general, apart from your health and lack of concentration, overall luck is quite good this month, and you can make good progress with your work. The negative aspects of the month are all transient in nature, so don't let minor obstacles get you down. Next month will be far better. Try not to take on too much for now. Manage your current tasks well but don't promise more than you can deliver.

BUSINESS - *Wealth Luck is Promising*

Wealth luck is promising and you may finally see some projects wrapping up. Don't forget to invoice for services rendered. You'll find money flowing in more easily this month, so collect while you have this kind of luck. Speed up the flow of wealth by displaying a sailing ship loaded with cargo sailing into the office from one of your auspicious directions. You may find yourself distracted by things outside of work which may cloud your judgment when it comes to decision-making in the business arena. This is not a good time for finalizing new initiatives. It is better to pause to think over complicated issues rather than to race ahead trying to get things done. While it is important to keep one step ahead of the competition, a bad decision can bring more problems than no decision at all. Don't let yourself be pressured into giving an answer on the spot.

LOVE & RELATIONSHIPS - *Promising*

Those of you in steady relationships have a good month in store. There is plenty to talk about with your partner in love and you have the chance to reconnect on many levels. You also find your partner or spouse bringing you many opportunities, whether directly or indirectly.

Single Dogs face a promising month when you could well find that someone special; but if you are looking to get into a relationship that lasts, overlook the superficial and go for what's inside. If you cannot connect on an intellectual level, chances of your romance lasting into the longer term are slim. You may be swept off your feet by someone who's unsuitable on the surface, but ditch the image game and listen to your heart; you could find true love this way.

9TH MONTH
Oct 8th - Nov 6th 2011

EMERGING VICTORIOUS OVER BAD VIBES

Your luck is strong this month and you have the triumphant number 1 star behind you. Whilst competition and rivalry is set to heat up, you can overcome whatever stands in your way of success provided you are determined enough. There are some sizeable changes to face this month, some truly life-changing, but take it all in your stride and trust what the Universe has in store for you. There are only good things ahead if you can overlook the difficult transition phase. Some of you could be looking at a relocation or a change in job even. Other Dogs may face a complete change of circumstance. This could be disconcerting at first, but as you get used to your new circumstances it could prove invigorating and liberating.

WORK & CAREER – *Making a Difference*

This month is bustling with activity. You're kept on your toes at work and your revitalized mind will welcome it. You find it difficult to sit still this month and are bustling with ideas you want to put into motion. Those of you in dead end jobs will be itching to throw caution to the winds and hand in that resignation letter you've been mulling over. Be brave about change this month. If you feel the time has come to move on, don't be afraid to do so. Hanging on to security and the past will only delay what's inevitable, and you'll be wondering why you didn't do something about it sooner. For others of you who are already sure you're headed in the right direction, this may be the time to make some significant changes to leapfrog to the next level. Don't just take what life thrusts at you; take control and make a difference of your own accord.

BUSINESS – Be Bold

This is not a month to be conservative; it is a time to be bold if you really want to make it big. In business, you are bound to go through both good and bad times. This is the beginning of the good times for you, so prepare yourself for the ride of your life.

An opportunity to work with someone you have admired for a long time could open up for you. Be sure you know the whole picture before being star struck and jumping in feet first, but this could be an opportunity of a lifetime. When you are offered a deal, no matter how attractive, don't sign anything without negotiating. The other party wants to work with you just as much as you them, so don't sell yourself cheap.

LOVE & RELATIONSHIPS – *Self-Centered*

You may tend to be rather self-centered this month, but as long as you are aware of this you can keep your admirers while playing top dog. Avoid getting involved in a relationship you don't think will last into the long term, as extricating yourself later on could be messy. Be prepared to face some big decisions this month. You could be thinking of ending a relationship or it could come to a natural end if you and your partner have drifted your separate ways. Don't cling on to the past; the energies this month encourage you to look onward into the future and your future looks very bright; so anything that happens is likely to be for the best. Those of you who are married however should not be so cavalier in your attitude. Make time for each other if you've been busy; quality time will go a long way to revitalizing your marriage.

EDUCATION – *Increase in Confidence*

Your interests may be changing. You may start liking a subject you used to dread or find difficult. Or you may suddenly become very good at something you thought you were hopeless at before. This gives you a renewed motivation to perform well, boosting your self-confidence and esteem.

10TH MONTH
Nov 7th - Dec 6th 2011

NEW BLUE OCEANS FOR YOUR BUSINESS

What a lucky month for the Dog person! Your good fortune from last month continues with opportunities falling into your lap. While it may be tempting to go after many things at once, keep your focus, because following up properly on one or two will land you more success than to have a foot in everything. You're raring to go and those of you in business have many unchartered oceans to sail and territories to conquer. When the competition heats up, don't look to beat them at their game using their strategies. Turn away and forge a completely new path in a brand new direction. Be innovative and clever when making plans. We are in a new world and those of you who can adapt quickly will benefit the most. Your wealth star gets enhanced this month, so it does suggest that there is a vein of prosperity waiting to be tapped. Your job is to find the best way.

WORK & CAREER – *In Your Element*

This is a most promising time at work. You're in your element. You're energetic and addictive, getting along with everybody. This makes you the perfect candidate for a whole variety of tasks that crop up at the workplace. It is easy for you to become the darling of the boss this way.

You have a flair for conversation, so don't get overly glued to your computer screen. Get to know what everyone else is up to in the office, make some friends and see how you can contribute more organically to the whole operation. Keep your focus and don't take things too slowly. Things happen quickly this month; don't stay satisfied with mediocre results because you have the potential to become a real star.

BUSINESS - *Follow Your Heart*

Luck is on your side so you can afford to take some risks and play up the stakes. If you are in an industry which requires lots of creativity, make sure you're personally involved in the creative process. Your tongue is sharp so whenever a debate is called for, chances are you'll win. But don't argue for the sake of arguing. Learn to recognize when you are both on the same side. You may have a tendency to be power hungry. If you want others to respect you, earn that respect. Don't demand that others listen to you; instead, use your intelligence to win them around. Be open to new ideas no matter how outlandish they sound at first. What works could surprise you. Don't go just with your head this month; follow your heart.

LOVE & RELATIONSHIPS – *Sparks Fly!*
Sparks fly this month when it comes to love, passion and romance! Everything about this month is exciting. You crave intimacy and chances are you'll have no trouble finding it; if not within your current relationship, then outside of it. If your current union is important to you, protect it by carrying or wearing the **double happiness symbol**. Try to make your partner do the same. Watch out for predatory third parties who may try to seduce you. You are susceptible this month to whoever offers you the physical excitement you yearn for.

EDUCATION – *Recognition Luck*
You have plenty of recognition luck this month so don't be surprised if more attention than usual is being showered on you. Your life may be so full it leaves you no time of your own at all. But this is the kind of month when it is better to go with the flow and see where the tide takes you. Don't try to make too many plans in advance, as chances are they'll get changed before they happen.

11TH MONTH
Dec 7th - Jan 5th 2012

ENDING THE YEAR ON A VERY HIGH NOTE

This is a wonderfully exciting month indeed! Everything good that's been suggesting itself has the chance to happen this month. Whatever you've wanted to achieve can get achieved. You just need to want it bad enough! Wealth luck in particular is spectacular, so get your entrepreneurial cap on right away. The most brilliant of ideas may start off seeming impractical, but if you believe in something enough and put in the effort to making it happen, the universe could well surprise you! There are many reasons to rejoice this month, and your happiness will come not just from work and business, but from your personal life as well. And you may surprise yourself when you realize the achievement of another person can be even more satisfying than your own success.

WORK & CAREER - *Promotion Luck*

This is a brilliant time at work when people take notice of you. All your proposals and ideas are well received, so feel free to be as forthcoming as you like. You may be given the chance to apply a different skill in your work, making your job more multi-dimensional and more interesting. You may also be put in a position of leadership. A promotion is highly possible. Because income luck is good, you may also get a raise. But don't get greedy and press for more money. The harder you work and the less you ask for, the more you will be remunerated.

BUSINESS - *Growth & Expansion*

Cutting lucrative business deals comes naturally to you this month. Go with the flow. You will know instinctively if something feels right. This is a good time to enter into win-win joint ventures, expand your business or launch new initiatives. You can afford to think big. The bolder you are, the greater your chances of big success. While there is much good fortune on your side, don't put all your eggs in one basket. There is always the outside factor that's unaccounted for that could bring unexpected results.

There's a lot you want to get done this month, but as one person, you can only take on so much. Make the best use of your team and empower them to work on your behalf. Learn to trust the people who work for you. If you allow them more freedom to do their jobs, you'll be pleasantly surprised at what they are capable of.

LOVE & RELATIONSHIPS - *Cozy*

A cozy time for the Dog person looking for romance. You find yourself in an amiable mood and enjoy the company of others. Flirting comes naturally and you will have as much romance as you want. This is a time when you call the shots in your relationships. You ooze charm and others are just clamoring to please you. Remember to return the favor if your partner does something sweet for you. If you are in a one-sided relationship, the good times may just come to an abrupt halt.

EDUCATION - *Friendships Feature Strongly*

Friends feature strongly in your life right now. Working in a group will bring good results this month. Sharing ideas and having discussions will improve your rate of learning. Apart from schoolwork, it is also important to give yourself relaxation time with your friends. Continue to keep up a good working pace, but leave time for enjoyment as well. Competition luck is good this month; if you are involved in a competitive sport, you will do well over the next four weeks.

12TH MONTH
Jan 6th - Feb 3rd 2012

GETTING RID OF THE BAD APPLES IN YOUR BASKET

The violent star makes an appearance bringing some danger of robbery and losing money. You could also be let down or even betrayed by someone you consider a friend. It pays to be more careful this month. Don't take your personal or home security for granted, and don't place your trust in others so easily, especially if you don't know them very well. At work, there may be one or two bad apples making trouble for everyone. For those of you working among them, it helps to be savvy. Don't let them politic or make trouble for you. For Dogs in business, you may have a troublesome employee in your midst. Deal with them carefully; this is not a good time to confront or condemn.

WORK & CAREER - *Out of Your Comfort Zone*

There may be significant developments at work that kick you out of your comfortable inertia. This could cause events to unfold one of two ways. You could find yourself out of your depth, or you could really find your forte and impress all the right people. The good news is that you are totally in control of your destiny here. You have the ability to seize this opportunity and make it a fantastic one for yourself, or you could fall flat on your face. But it is all up to you and how committed you are to make something of yourself. Watch out for colleagues making trouble for you. There may be one or two jealous of your success. Make sure you have a **Rooster** on your workdesk to protect you against becoming a victim of office politics.

BUSINESS - *Good Opportunities*
There is good money luck in your chart this month. Some good business opportunities are likely to come your way. However, be careful when dealing with individuals you do not know well. There is a danger of having the wool pulled over your eyes. Don't be overly trusting, and do your research before entering into a venture. If you are astute about it, you can get yourself some good deals this month. Use your intelligence and do not take your decisions lightly. Get involved in your operations and make it a point to know in detail the goings-on in your business.

LOVE & RELATIONSHIPS - *Chance Encounters*
Chance encounters could lead to interesting developments in your love life. Your sex life gets a boost but beware that your feelings don't cloud your

judgment. If you have other responsibilities, don't let a passionate love life make you abandon them. Family may get in the way when it comes to your relationships. Instead of letting this rile you, ask why they disapprove. They may be able to see something that you can't. You can be somewhat vulnerable to advances for suitors that may not have the best of intentions. Watch you're with the right person by refraining from jumping into a relationship without checking things out first.

EDUCATION - *Stand Up for Yourself*
Success breeds jealousy and this month you could become the target of a disgruntled bully. Stand up for yourself when others try to be funny with you. Don't take any nonsense form anyone. At the same time, don't pick a fight when you don't have to. Avoid making enemies, but don't tolerate them either. It is important not to let a classmate get the better of you, or they may try it again. Stand up for yourself.

Important Feng Shui Updates for 2011

Part 6

If you have been following the advice given in these Fortune & Feng Shui books on annual feng shui updates, you are already familiar with the time dimension of feng shui which protects against negative luck each year.

This requires overall cleansing and re-energizing of the energy of the home to prepare for the coming of a new year, while simultaneously making placement changes to accommodate a new pattern of chi distribution. Getting rid of old items and replacing with specially made new remedial cures that are in tune with the year's chi brings pristine and fresh new luck into the home.

It is vital to anticipate and quickly suppress the source of malicious chi brought by the new feng shui winds of the year, as this ensures that bad chi originating in afflicted sectors never have a chance to gather, accumulate, grow strong and then ripen in a burst of bad luck! With powerful remedies in place, this will not happen, thereby keeping residents safe from misfortune that can be unsettling and heartbreaking.

Severe bad luck that brings despair can happen to anyone. Sometimes, even in the midst of some personal triumphant moment, your world can suddenly crumble before you. Last year for instance, the world witnessed the incredibly sad falling apart of the marriages of **Kate Winslet** and **Sandra Bullock** soon after they each had reached the pinnacle of their profession by winning the Oscar for Best Actress. Kate had won in 2009 and Sandra in 2010.

Both had gushed and thanked their husbands in their acceptance speeches, obviously unaware of destructive energies lurking within their homes. Both husbands - for whatever reasons - were looking for satisfaction elsewhere outside their marriages! Kate's husband, noted director Sam Mendes' eyes had already started roving in 2009... but the marriage had fallen apart only in 2010 when the grief-bringing star of infidelity made its appearance. Both actresses do not believe in luck... and it is safe to assume they are too busy to have the time to pause, and arrange for the placement of feng shui cures in their homes.

Those not following time dimension feng shui from these books are unlikely to have known that last year 2010 was a year when the external romance star of peach blossom was lurking in every household, creating the potential to cause havoc in marriages! It was vital last year to place cures in the home to protect against outsider third party interference. Sandra Bullock and Kate Winslet are just two of the high profile victims of the star of *External Peach Blossom*! They are exquisitely beautiful ladies, but both of their marriages unraveled in March of 2010!

It is therefore so important that each time we cross into a new year, we should note the particular ailments and afflictions of the year, and then carefully bring in the antidotes so we can sail through the year without having to endure the consequences of bad feng shui, which of course can manifest in different ways. No matter how it manifests, bad luck always brings distress, heartbreak and a sense of helplessness. Why go through this kind of unhappiness when you can prevent or reduce it?

Each year there will be the same kinds of afflictions bringing illness, accidents, robbery, quarrels and misfortune, but these afflictions change location each year and vary in strength from year to year. So we need to systematically suppress these "*staples of bad luck*" first.

Then there are the disturbing stars of misfortune - these too need to be neutralized mainly with element therapy so that they do not cast their ill influence onto your luck.

In some years, there can be some hazardous or dangerous alignment of energies we need to be careful of, and these also need to be addressed. For instance, we have already told you about the four pillars of clashing elements bringing severe quarrelsome energy that can get violent.

Incense and aromas are an effective way of transcending time and space, blending heaven and earth energies to chase away all the afflictions that bring disaster, setbacks and accidents. Although invisible, incense offering rituals when done correctly can overcome obstacles especially obstacles that may be blocking your luck. The use of incense is part of spiritual feng shui - the third dimension of inner feng shui that can make a great difference to allowing good fortune into your life.

The regular infusion of incense (with some smoke) clears the pathway for good chi energy to flow into your home; and symbolic placements then work more effectively to create the lucky ambience you need. Home energy then becomes harmonious and benevolent, blending beautifully with new patterns of chi formations that are flowing through your home. Try infusing your space with the special blend of sandalwood or pine incense and feel the difference instantly!

Focusing on your house feng shui from this perspective will help you enjoy a better year irrespective of how good or how bad the indications for the year may be. The use of incense can go a long way to subduing afflicted energy hidden in corners of the house that affect your animal sign in any year.

This dissolves afflictions building up in corners of homes and strengthens the placement cures you use to suppress bad feng shui.

Misfortunes, illness, accidents and things going wrong always worse seem worse when they catch you unawares. You really do not want to have to face the prospect of losing your job, your home, your good name, your child, your lover or your spouse, and these are just some of the misfortunes that are brought by the bad stars of the feng shui chart each year.

It is only when afflictive energies are effectively suppressed that whatever bad event may occur can be prevented. This is the wonderful promise and benefit of creating good timely feng shui in the home. And when divine assistance is invoked through the wearing of powerful amulets and sacred talismans the remedies become even more powerful. This brings harmony and smooth sailing through the year.

Luck is never static

Luck always occurs in cycles and the key to continuing good fortune is to know when the luck of your home is at its peak and when it requires extra protection. When important areas of the house gets hit by misfortune-bringing stars, everyone living within gets hurt. In the same way when these same areas are visited by lucky stars, everyone in the house enjoys good luck.

To what degree this incidence of good and bad luck affects residents depends also on their personal outlook for the year. Cycles of luck affect different people in different ways and this is one reason why it can be so beneficial to analyze how the year affects your animal sign. Here we are not just talking about 12 animal signs.

Consider the infinite variations of each individual's pattern of luck when you factor in the two sets of elements in the four sets of birth data - Year, Month, Day and Hour of Birth... then factor in the house, the locations of the main door, the bedroom, the dining and living area.

Factor in also the changing energies of the year as well as the energy of the people who surround you, make up your circle of family and friends ... and you will be awed by the mathematical combinations of chi that are affecting you every single moment!

We cannot take care of everything that affects our luck, but we sure can take care of enough to ensure a pretty good and smooth year. And once we are assured that we have been adequately protected, we can then turn our attention to maximizing good fortune for the year... Success, Love, Satisfaction with Life, Money, Wealth, Career highs, Contentment... and a lot more can then be induced to manifest into our lives. This depends on what we want, what we energize for and how we enhance our bedrooms, work spaces and living areas. It is really easier than you think! Just protect against bad luck and energize for good luck.

You must first protect your **main door** and your **bedroom**. Where these two vital spots of your house are located must be protected against bad numbers or bad stars. Afflictive energy can be illness or misfortune numbers, hostile or robbery stars. These can, together with other kinds of negative energy, cause loss of some kind.

Someone could force you into litigation - this is something that will happen more often than usual this year; you might suffer a break-up of an important relationship - this too is unfortunately being fanned by the destructive patterns of elements this year.
Severe bad luck or loss, when it manifests, is always traumatic. Feng shui corrections offer the solutions

to avoiding or at least diminishing the chances of negativities happening. Knowing feng shui enables you to anticipate a potentially problematic year; and then to do something about it.

> ## Correcting and suppressing bad energy is rarely difficult. But it requires a bit of effort.

What you need to do is to systematically go through each of the nine sectors of your home - mentally dividing your home into a three-by-three sector grid that corresponds to eight compass directions with a center.

The next step is to study the year's charts; first the Annual Feng Shui chart which pinpoints the afflicted parts of the home, then the 24 mountain charts which show the "*stars*", both lucky and unlucky, that also influence the year's distribution of luck, and finally, the year's four pillars chart.

It is the collective and unified analysis of these indications that point to what needs to be done to safeguard the feng shui of any abode.

Suppressing
Flying Star Afflictions for the Year

Traditionally, one of the more important things to update prior to each new year is to find the new locations for all the afflictive star numbers and then to deal with each of them. These yearly afflictions are the same each year, but their strength and severity vary from year to year, depending on where they are. The element of each affliction interacts with the element of the sector they fly into.

In some years, the misfortune star number of five yellow a.k.a. *wu wang* can be really strong, while in some years, they are weaker.

In 2011, the *wu wang* flies to the East, where its Earth element is strongly suppressed by the Wood element here. The 2011 *wu wang* is thus not as strong as it was in the previous year when it occupied the Southwest. There the Earth element of the Southwest strengthened the *wu wang*.

In 2011 therefore, we are not so afraid of this otherwise feared star. In spite of this, it is still advisable to keep it under control in case someone in the house is going through weak Life Force year or whose Spirit Essence may be lacking.

Remedies against the Wu Wang

It is necessary to place the traditional remedies to suppress *wu wang* in the East, because it is an unpleasant star number whose effect can suddenly

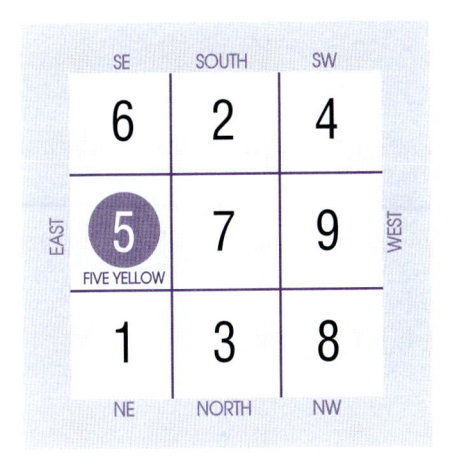

	SE	SOUTH	SW
	6	2	4
EAST	**5** FIVE YELLOW	7	9	WEST
	1	3	8
	NE	NORTH	NW

manifest bad things if your bedroom happens to be affected by it OR if it is also being hit by some secret poison arrow unknown to you. This acts as a catalyst for the *wu wang* to erupt; likewise, if the Wood element in the East gets inadvertently weakened for whatever reason, then the *wu wang can get* strengthened. The *wu wang* blocks success and affects the luck of the eldest son of the family, bringing great distress. To be safeguarded, it is advisable to place the remedy specially designed for the *wu wang* of 2011 and place in the East sectors of the main rooms of the home, including the living room and other areas where your family spend time. Place the cures on a sideboard or table, not on the floor!

Five Element Pagoda with Tree of Life

In 2011, we are recommending the five element pagoda that comes with a wood base and decorated with an all-powerful Tree of Life that grows from the base of the pagoda right to the tip. There are three pairs of birds on the branches of the tree of life.

> The birds that sit on the Tree of Life bring opportunities from the cosmic constellations and legend has it they attract exactly the kind of luck a household needs.

From the leaves of the tree hang glittering jewels which signify the treasures of the earth, the element that symbolizes wealth and prosperity in 2011. This powerful five element pagoda is actually a transforming tool which turns the all-powerful *wu wang* into a wealth-enhancing tool. Note that this powerful pagoda synchronizes extremely well with the energies of 2011 and 2012 when the *wu wang* flies to the Wood sectors of the compass. It is usually not used during other years.

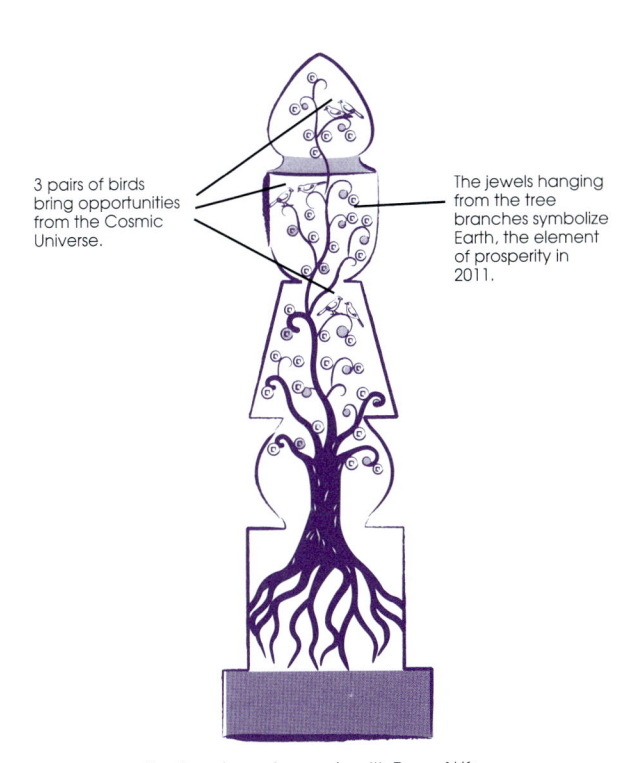

3 pairs of birds bring opportunities from the Cosmic Universe.

The jewels hanging from the tree branches symbolize Earth, the element of prosperity in 2011.

The **five element pagoda** with Tree of Life transforms the *wu wang* into a wealth-bringing star.

Metal Bell with Tree of Life

Another very beneficial cure for the 2011 *wu wang* is the powerful Bell which is also made of metal but has a wooden mallet, so the sound created is more mellow and lower than that of an all-metal bell. The handle of the bell is made of wood; and on the bell itself there is again the amazing tree of life to strengthen the Wood chi of the East; and the tree also has 6 birds on its branches; and with jewels on its leaves to signify wealth luck.

This transforms the five element bell into an empowering tool which, even as it suppresses the *wu wang*, is simultaneously sending out powerful vibrations each time the sounds of the bell are created. This way, the bell utilizes the *wu wang* to attract great good fortune opportunities and it is by placing a tree of life with 6 birds that gives it these attributes. We have also embossed the *dependent arising mantra* onto both the **five element bell** and **pagoda**.

The **Metal Bell with wooden handle** is another enhancing tool that simultaneously suppresses the *wu wang*.

This powerful mantra greatly empowers these cures! Those wanting to wear these powerful symbols over the two years 2011 and 2012 can consider wearing either the pagoda or the bell with the tree design to safeguard themselves from the wu wang.

> Those born in Dog years need to be extra wary in June, as this is when the *wu wang* flies into your month chart. But because the Dog location in the NW is a Metal sector, the *wu wang* is not as strong here as elsewhere. Nevertheless, it is still beneficial to place the five element pagoda with the tree of life here.

Misfortunes caused by the *wu wang* in 2011 will not be as severe as in other years but they are still aggravating. It can cause problems with employees or act as a catalyst for other kinds of bad luck to occur, so do suppress its negative effect. This year's cure also uses the inherent strength of the *wu wang* to transform bad luck into something good.

If you reside in a room located in the East sector of your house, place the pagoda inside your bedroom. Make sure it is in place before February 3rd which is the start of the Lunar New Year 2011. It is important not to undertake renovations on the East side of the house through the year.

Avoid all kinds of demolition or digging work although there are some feng shui masters who say that building works are not harmful, arguing that anything productive will not harm the household. We disagree with this as the *wu wang* should not be activated by any kind of building. This only strengthens it.

Planting a tree in the East is however very auspicious, especially if you do this on **February 4th**, the day of the **lap chun**!

Other Afflictions of the 2011 Chart

The illness causing star flies to the South in 2011. This is an Earth element star flying into a Fire sector, so here, the illness star gets considerably strengthened, making it a serious threat to residents, but especially for anyone residing in the South sector of the house; but the illness star affects everyone if it is where the main door into the house is located.

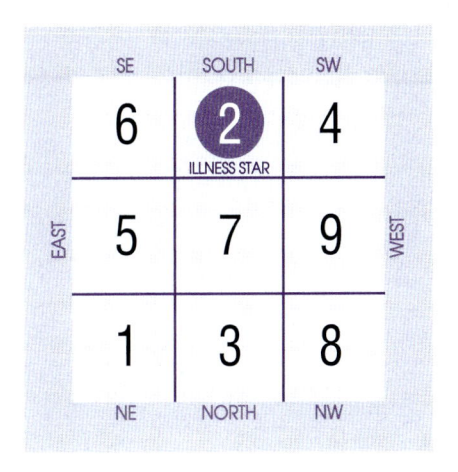

SE	SOUTH	SW
6	2 ILLNESS STAR	4
EAST 5	7	9 WEST
1	3	8
NE	NORTH	NW

Any house that faces or sits South will find that residents within are more vulnerable to catching viruses and falling ill more easily. Try using another door to enter and leave the house by, to avoid overactivating the South.

Should the main door of the house be in the South, the constant opening and closing of the door will energize the star, making it more likely to bring illness into the house and this is pronounced during the months of March and December when the month stars mirror that of the year hence bringing a double whammy to afflicted sectors.

If your door is facing South, it is a good idea to use another door located in another sector (if possible) especially during these two months.

If this is not possible then it is necessary to exhaust the Earth element of the illness star placing something metallic or made of wood here.

It is necessary also to remove all Earth element items such as crystals, porcelain vases or stone objects from the South. Also keep lights in the South dim to reduce Fire element energy.

Cures for the Illness Star of 2011

Over the years, we have found that the best way to suppress illness energy brought by the intangible flying star 2 is to suppress its negative effect with a wu lou shaped container made of metal - either in brass or steel. To the Chinese, the wu lou is a container for keeping herbal cures, so that over the years it has come to signify medicinal qualities. Many of China's favorite deities and especially the **Goddess of Mercy, Kuan Yin** are usually depicted carrying a small wu lou shaped little bottle that is said to contain healing nectar.

Placing a large **wu lou** in the South generates invisible healing energies for both physical as well as mental afflictions. It is as good as medicine, and in fact, it is also a very good idea to place a small wu lou by your bedside so that it exudes healing energies even as you sleep. This is good feng shui!

You can also invoke the help of the powerful healing Buddha, also known as the **Medicine Buddha**. This is the blue-bodied Buddha whose image and mantra create so many blessings that the residents of any home that displays the Medicine Buddha image in any way at all, especially in the sector where the illness flying star is located, ill enjoy good health, rarely if ever falling sick. It is a good idea in 2011 to have an image of **Medicine Buddha** placed on a table top in the **North** part of any room where you spend a great deal of time.

Those feeling poorly in 2011 should also wear **Medicine Buddha bracelets** or our specially designed **moving mantra watches** - the only watches of its kind in the world! We brought out the first such moving mantra watch last year and they have since helped so many people that we have extended our range to include a watch with the healing image of the Medicine Buddha. Wearing such a watch is like having prayers being constantly recited for your good health. It is truly amazing how far technology has progressed. To us, it makes sense to utilize all the technical advances that have made so many wonderful new products possible. Many of the advances in technology have made feng shui very easy to practice.

Wear the **watch** with the healing image of **Medicine Buddha** to protect against the illness star of 2011.

The Quarrelsome Hostile Star flies to the North in 2011

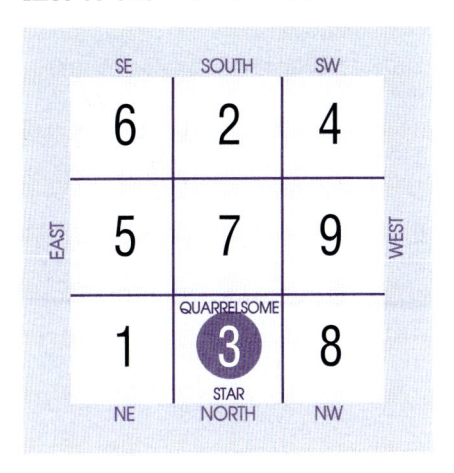

	SE	SOUTH	SW	
	6	2	4	
EAST	5	7	9	WEST
	1	QUARRELSOME **3** STAR	8	
	NE	NORTH	NW	

This is a Wood element star flying into a Water element sector. As such, this noisy, litigation-bringing star number is both strong and harder to overcome. It is dangerous and aggravating and very capable of causing anyone staying in the North sector a great deal of problems. This is the major affliction affecting anyone having a bedroom in the North sector in 2011.

You are likely to be more easily stressed out and this will affect your productivity levels. For some, it can even create obstacles that block your luck. At its worst, the effect of this affliction is to be hit with someone bringing you into litigation, causing you no end of aggravating pressure and inconveniences, or someone getting violent with you. This star brings a pervasive feeling of hostility, short tolerance levels and a great deal of impatience. There will be arguments, fights and misunderstandings for everyone directly hit by it.

Unfortunately for anyone having a bedroom in the **North** sector of the house, the **quarrelsome star 3 is made stronger** this year because its Wood Element is produced even more by the Water element of the North.

As a Wood element star, the best way to subdue its effect is to exhaust it with Fire Element energy. Anything that suggests Fire is an excellent cure, so bright lights and the color red are excellent remedies. Hence, because the North is associated with water energy, the danger is enhanced so remedying it is vital.

Carry the Red Dragon Amulet to subdue quarrelsome energies through the year.

If you are afflicted by this star, make sure you are not hurt by it in any way by carrying the **Red Dragon amulet**. This brings luck while keeping the number 3 star subdued. Note that this amulet has the Dragon carrying a sword in its right claw, as this helps overcome all the clashing elements of the year.

The Violent Star 7 attracts bad people into the home

The Violent Star 7 which attracts bad people into the home is in the center of the chart this year, where it is symbolically locked up, hence reducing its influence. This is an affliction which hurts most when it occupies

	SE	SOUTH	SW
	6	2	4
EAST	5	7 VIOLENT STAR	9	WEST
	1	3	8
	NE	NORTH	NW

one of the outer sectors of any building, but trapped in the center, its negative impact is less severe.

> The number 7 star number is a **Metal element number** and with the center being an Earth sector, here we have a situation of **Earth producing Metal**, so while it may be hemmed in in the center, it is nevertheless **troublesome**. It is a number that causes loss through being cheated or robbed.

A good way of keeping this affliction under wraps is simply to place a small sideboard in the center of the house, place seven pieces of metal within and then lock it up. This symbolically "locks up" the number 7 star very effectively. At the same time, have a **Blue Rhino with a 6-tusk Elephant** near the entrance into the home. However, should any of you be feeling vulnerable with the burglary star in the center of the home, you can safeguard yourself by carrying the **Blue Rhino & Elephant** or using it as a hanging on your bags or hung in the car. It is good practice to stay protected against encountering bad people who would want to harm you. Use the **Blue Rhino & Elephant protector** as this continues to be an effective cure in 2011. It is a highly respected cure against the potential violence of the 7.

Note that the problem with the number 7 star in 2011 is that being in the center of the feng shui chart, the number 7 can potentially spread its influence into any part of the house, hence it is necessary to keep it well under control. The best is to literally "*lock it up*", otherwise it simply plays havoc with house security. It is very inconvenient and even dangerous when the 7 star number strikes.

In 2011 the God of the Year cannot be ignored

The Tai Sui is important because this year it directly faces the *Star of Natural Disaster* in the West. This is a 24 mountain star that sits between the two stars of *three killings*! That there are such intensive negative stars directly confronting the Tai Sui is not good for the year. It suggests a battle, and when a battle takes place, there is always collateral damage!

Especially when they are read against the background of the year's clashing elements in the four pillars; these signs collectively indicate clear and present danger. How the dangers of the year manifest will vary in timing and severity for different houses and different countries; but generally, an afflicted Tai Sui means that the wars of the world currently being waged on several fronts are unlikely to decline. There is also no let up in the occurrence of natural disasters.

Do be extra mindful of the Tai Sui in 2011. Avoid confronting it. Avoid facing East and make extra efforts not to "*disturb*" its location, the East sector of the house. This sector must be kept quiet as noise activates the Tai Sui and incurs its wrath. Also avoid digging, banging or renovating this side of the home.

It is beneficial to place a well-executed art piece of the beautiful Pi Yao in the East as this celestial creature is excellent for appeasing the Tai Sui. The Pi Yao always brings good feng shui and it is for this reason that you will find many artistic variations of this auspicious creature all over China and Hong Kong.

It is a great favorite with people who believe in feng shui. It brings exceptional good fortune into the home. For 2011, a Pi Yao made in Earth element material is preferred, as this element signifies wealth luck. So crystal or ceramic Pi Yao or one made in *liu li* medium would be excellent.

It is important for everyone whose bedroom is in the **East,** or whose sitting direction while working is facing or sitting East, to place the **Pi Yao** near you.

Place a **Pi Yao** in the East sector of the home to appease the Tai Sui who resides there in 2011.

Part 6 : Important Feng Shui Updates for 2011

It does not matter if the Pi Yao is standing or sitting but it should appear proud and majestic looking. The more beautiful looking the Pi Yao is, the better it is to display in the house to appease the Tai Sui. This advice applies to anyone irrespective of their animal sign.

The place of the Tai Sui is taken very seriously in feng shui.

It is emphasized in the *Treatise on Harmonizing Times and Distinguishing Directions* compiled under the patronage of the Qianlong Emperor during his reign in the mid-Eighteenth century and any Master practicing feng shui in China or Hong Kong always ensures the Tai Sui is respected and thus taken account of in their updating process.

The Emperor Qiang Lung inspired Treatise states that the locations where the Tai Sui resides and where the Tai Sui has just vacated are **lucky** locations. So note that in 2011, the locations of East and NE1 are considered lucky, benefiting from the lingering energy of the Tai Sui. Those having their rooms in these locations will enjoy the patronage and protection of the Tai Sui in 2011. The Treatise further explains that it is unlucky to reside in the location where the Tai Sui is progressing towards i.e. clockwise on the astrology compass. In 2011 this means the SE1 location; it is unlucky to directly confront the Tai Sui's residence. It is unlucky to "*face*" the Tai Sui because this is deemed rude, so the advice for 2011 is to not to directly face East.

In 2011, never forget to avoid confronting the Tai Sui. **Do not face East this year** even if this is your success direction under the Kua formula of personalized lucky directions.

Those who forget and inadvertently face the Tai Sui run the risk of offending the Tai Sui. This brings obstacles to your work life. Your road to achieving success gets constantly interrupted and for some, supporters can turn into adversaries.

Carry the **Tai Sui Amulet** to subdue the Grand Duke Jupiter for the Year 2011.

In 2011, the West of every building is afflicted by the Three Killings

This affliction brings three severe misfortunes associated with loss, grief and sadness. Its location each year is charted according to the animal sign that rules the year. Thus in 2011 it flies to the West because the Rabbit belongs to the Triangle of Affinity made up of the Rabbit, Sheep and Boar; with the Rabbit occupying a cardinal direction (East).

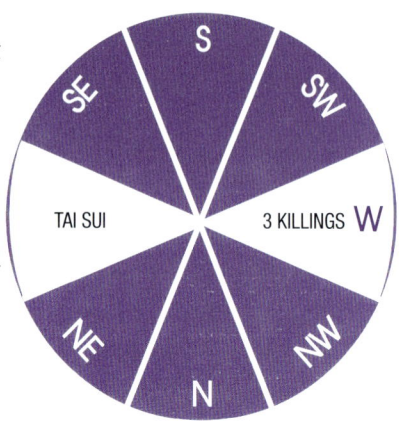

The Three Killings is thus in the West, the direction that is directly opposite the Rabbit. This feng shui aggravation affects only primary directions, so unlike other feng shui afflictions, the direct bad effects of the three killings are felt over a larger area of the house.

The three killings bring three kinds of loss; the loss of one's good reputation, the loss of a loved one and the loss of wealth. When you suffer a sudden reversal of fortune, it is usually due to being hit by the three killings. In 2011, the three killings reside in the West where it poses some danger to the young daughters of the family. Anyone occupying the West would be vulnerable to being hit by the three killings.

For everyone whose bedroom and/or main door face West or are located in the West sector of your home, please get the celestial protectors - the Chi Lin, the Fu Dog and the Pi Yao - preferably made colorful and with a fierce expression. Place them close together, either on a coffee table or on a sideboard; get them in brass and enamel. For them to be effective, some texts refer also to the three different deities traditionally

SE	SOUTH	SW
6	2	4
5 (EAST)	7	9 — 3 KILLINGS (WEST)
1	3	8
NE	NORTH	NW

seated on their backs, but as a feng shui cure, they are as effective on their own or with the deities, although the secret is to make certain they have their different *implements* with them, as these enable them to symbolically overcome the afflictions.

> The **Sword** on the back of the **Pi Yao** protects against loss of wealth. The **Lasso** on the back of the **Chi Lin** to protects against loss of loved one. The **Steel Hook** on the back of the **Fu Dog** protects against loss of good name. The hook is a very powerful implement which also "*hooks in wealth luck*".

These three celestial guardians are extremely effective; but this year an old Taoist master has advised to also add in the implements, and confirmed that as feng shui cures, they work best when new. This ensures that their energy is strong. Try not to use antique images as feng shui cures. These are usually surrounded by tired chi. Feng shui remedies must possess fresh new energy to be strong with vitality chi.

Antique furniture decorated with celestials can be lovely to look at, but they rarely make effective cures. They can however generate auspicious chi after they are cleansed of lingering yin vibes. Use a dry cloth with sea or crystal salt to wipe off stale chi and they should be fine.

Do this cleansing ritual at least once a year. The month before the Lunar New Year is a good time. The energy of the three killings can sometimes stick on to furniture, especially those that have animals or human images painted onto them. Always use rock salt to wipe off lingering bad chi. Those of who may want to stay protected from the *three killings* and prevent them from overwhelming you when you are out and about this year can also hang the three celestials amulet on your bags.

Carry the **3 Celestial Guardian with Implements Keychain** to protect you from 3 Killings.

Part 6 : Important Feng Shui Updates for 2011

Those staying in the West sectors of the house could experience bad dreams and nightmares. The three celestial guardians placed on a cabinet along the west wall of the room should cure this. If you have a window in the bedroom, place the three celestials there even if it is not the West wall. The presence of the **three celestial guardians** is a powerful protective cosmic force.

Subduing Right & Strengthening Left of the Dog's Luck

The Dog benefits from one of the stars of the 24 mountains in 2011. This circle of cosmic energy brings the lucky *Small Auspicious Star* to the Dog's left and this should be energized with the presence of bright lights.

The Dog is sitting on the *Star of Yearly Conflict,* making it susceptible to being somewhat aggressive this year, and on its left is the *Star of Small Auspicious* and to the right the *Star of Three Killings*. This star on the right is an affliction associated with the Rooster, so it suggests that this is a year when there is underlying tension coming from anyone close to you born in the sign of the Rooster

To strengthen the 24 mountain star of *Small Auspicious*, you can enhance the NW with bright

THE 24 MOUNTAIN STARS CHART OF 2011

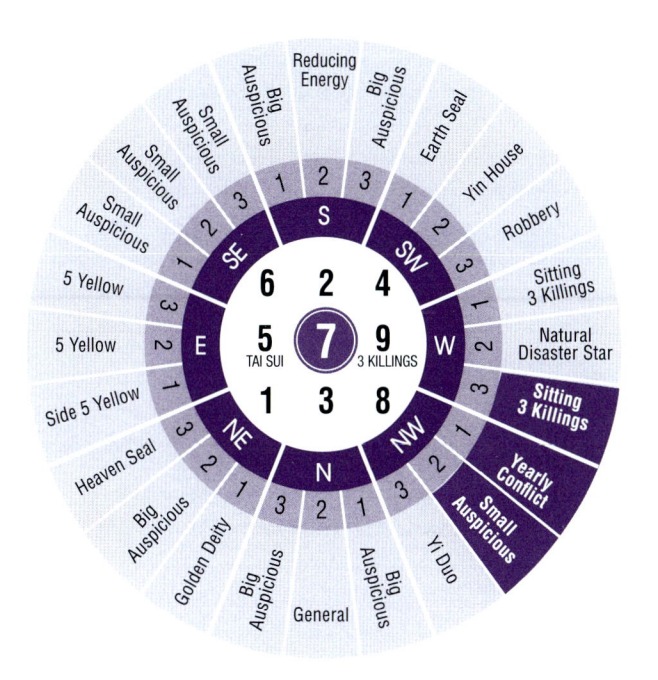

The Dog's NW2 location is flanked by Sitting 3 Killings on one side and Small Auspicious Star in 2011.

Part 6 : Important Feng Shui Updates for 2011

lights, and to subdue the *three killings,* place the three celestial guardians in the West location. It is important to get the location just right, so stand in the center of the room which you want to activate the stars of small auspicious in the NW. Then using a good 24 mountain compass, mark out the exact spot that corresponds to the NW 1 direction. Here, install a bright light shining upwards.

Remember that placement feng shui works best when there is accuracy of compass readings, so do invest in a good compass and learn to take accurate compass readings.

Scents to Transcend the Cosmic Fields of Energy

Aromas such as lavender diffused into space and incense created with pine and other aromas are powerful mediums that can be used to transcend the cosmic fields of energy that surround us. We have spent the past year talking about the third dimension of feng shui, and the use of aromas is one of the more common ways used by Masters skilled in the spiritual and shamanistic aspects of feng shui practice.

At its most basic, joss sticks are used during the Wealth God welcoming rituals performed during the night before the Lunar New Year; during such rituals very pungent and strong smells such as sandalwood are used. These cut through the energy of space connecting heaven with earth chi. Incense is also used to symbolically cleanse anything you bring into the house, from jewellery to furniture!

Scents can be used through the year. They are powerful for clearing the air of negatives and to suppress troublesome energies that bring aggravations which disturb the minds of residents. Aromas are associated with the transcendence of chi energy between cosmic realms of consciousness and are an advanced form of energy practices used in the old days by expert practitioners.

Aromas are powerful yet invisible instruments for dissolving concentrations of negative energy. All afflictions can be dissolved with ritualistic incense pujas, and there are other aromatic pujas that can manifest good fortune.

This can be infused into the air or burnt with charcoal. The latter is more powerful as this disperses obstacles faster and more efficiently. Do this once a week on a day that is lucky for you or on a day when you have a special meeting scheduled.

Activating the Trinity of Tien Ti Ren

In the year 2011, **all four primary directional locations** - North, South, East and West - are afflicted, as we have seen with the *Illness*, *Hostile*, *Five Yellow* and *Natural Disaster* star. Of the four, only the West location has the lucky 9 star number, but 9 in a Metal element sector always contains hidden dangers; so correcting and placing remedies to safeguard the cardinal locations of the house is extremely important in 2011.

The **four secondary directions** on the other hand, are indicating extremely lucky star numbers, with 8 leading the way as it flies into the patriarchal corner of Northwest, followed by the heavenly 6 in the opposite direction of Southeast. Then there is the *Victory Star* in the Northeast and the star of romance and scholarship in the Southwest in 2011.

With this kind of star number configurations, we also note that the Northeast/Southwest axis (which is the favorable axis of this current period of 8) has been blessed with the star of *Earth Seal* in the SW and the matching counterpart star of the *Heaven Seal* in the Northeast. The presence of these heaven and earth stars are indicative of the need for the trinity of lucky cosmic forces to be present in the North and the South, the other set of axis direction which are showing a set of two *Big Auspicious* stars. In N1 and N3 and also in S1 and S3, we see here a quartet of important lucky stars brought by the circle of the 24 mountains.

In 2011, there is the strong indication of substantial changes taking place in the world which will **bring benefits to some** and **loss to others**. This is vital to understand, as the year itself is showing a set of four pillars which not only has **4 sets of clashing elements** but also **two yang and two yin pillars**. This suggests that the complementarily of cosmic forces is balanced. **Yin and yang are in balance**.

Good fortune manifests as growth, sudden windfalls and big transformations of luck that bring a "*house filled with jewels*" enabling one to "*wear the jade belt*" if the household successfully activates the trinity of *Tien Ti Ren*. In other words, there must be plentiful supply of heaven, earth and mankind energies! This is something that is beneficial to ensure at all times, but more so in 2011, where severe bad luck indications are balanced against equally powerful auspicious indications. So the important thing is to tap into the positive energies of the year, thereby getting onto the growth spiral. *Tien ti ren* is the key! Symbolically, just placing the words heaven and earth is often good enough to complement the presence of people within a home.

Mankind chi is the powerful yang chi that activates the yin earth chi and the cosmic heaven chi.

In the old days, wealthy households would always include miniature mountains to signify Earth, and also all the Deities of their faith - Taoism or Buddhism, the **8 Immortals** and the **18 Holy Beings** - all to signify heaven chi while at the same time imbuing their homes with activity and celebrations to signify mankind chi. This infusion of yang energy acts a catalyst to generate the presence of the powerful cosmic trinity.

In this way did wealthy households of the past live, and over the years, these practices came to signify the cultural underpinnings of the Chinese way of life. Thus one should not be surprised to note that many Chinese households believe that the blessing power of heaven is brought in by the presence of deities on their family altar. The family altar was always placed rather grandly, directly facing the front door. This signified the continuing presence of heaven luck. It was important to keep the family altars clean with offerings of food, lights, water, wine and incense made daily.

Wealthier households would even have professionals such as monks and holy mencome and recite prayers for the family at special dates in the year. These were daily rituals believed to keep the family patriarch safe and the household in a state of abundance. In other words, keeping their lifestyles secure.

In addition, good Earth chi was assured by the presence of mountains and rivers simulated in landscaped gardens around the family home and symbolized by **mountain scenery paintings** inside the home. Good feng shui also ensures good chi flows in abundance through the rooms and corridors of the house.

Finally, excellent mankind chi is kept flowing fresh and revitalizing yang energy.

Auspicious phrases and lucky rhyming couplets were placed as **artistic calligraphy** in important rooms of the house; this was the equivalent of today's very popular "*affirmation*s".

The Chinese have been living with these powerful affirmations for as long as anyone can remember, and there are literally thousands of such lucky phrases such as "*your wealth has arrived*" or "your luck is as long as the yellow river"... and so forth. These are popular sayings exchanged between families during festive seasons and during Chinese New Year. Anyone wanting to enjoy good fortune continuously must be mindful of the power generated by *tien ti ren* chi inside their homes. This is very timely for 2011 to help you benefit from the year.

In 2011 therefore, the three dimensions of feng shui - space and time as well as the dimension which engages the cosmic force within the self (the purest source of yang energy generated from within you) must all be present. In fact, this is a major secret of feng shui. This is the mankind chi that pulls heaven and earth chi together. Good mankind chi requires you to stay positive, to generate lucky aspirations and to anticipate good outcomes. Your expectations must be high. You can enhance the empowerment of your own self. This unlocks for you the strength of mankind luck - *ren* chi - which pulls time and space into a powerful whole. With this kind of attitude, you can then start to enhance the four lucky secondary directions with powerful enhancing placement feng shui.

Enhancing the Chi of 8 in the Northwest

The all-powerful and auspicious 8 flies to the place of the patriarch in 2011, bringing quite exceptional great good fortune to all the father figures of the world.

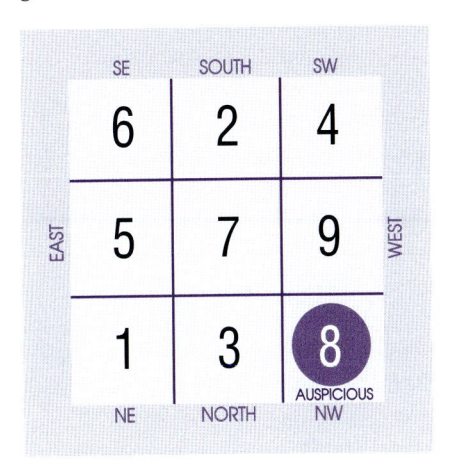

	SE	SOUTH	SW	
	6	2	4	
EAST	5	7	9	WEST
	1	3	8 AUSPICIOUS	
	NE	NORTH	NW	

Being located in the Northwest, the 8 Earth Star also gets very considerably strengthened, especially since it is flying to the NW from the center where it was located last year.

As an annual star number, the 8 is indeed very strong. It brings good relationship luck and it brings success and wealth. It is a powerful star at its zenith. What worked last year, the **crystal 8** embedded with real 24 carat gold, continues to work this year, so do display it in the Northwest of the house; or of your office.

But the crystal 8 becomes even more powerful when it is placed alongside a **crystal Ru Yi**, the **scepter of authority**. This is especially beneficial for Chief Executive Officers i.e. CEOs and bosses; in fact, anyone in a position of authority and power will benefit from the Ru Yi placed alongside the 8.

Those who want to boost their career luck should consider placing this powerful symbol of upward mobility in the NW corner of their home, office or home office. With the 8 flying into the NW, the Ru Yi placed next to the 8 becomes especially effective. Place the Ru Yi in the middle of the NW sector (i.e. NW2) as this is the auspicious part of this location.

Do note also that the Northwest 1 location belongs to your sign, that of the Dog, and hence it is definitely a very good idea to place an image of the Dog here to directly harness the power of 8 to benefit you. It is also excellent to activate the NW location with the abundant 8 water feature to jump start your luck in 2011.

Activating the Power of Heavenly 6 in the Southeast

The number 6, a lucky white star usually associated with the cosmic energies of heaven, flies to the Southeast in 2011, directly facing the Northwest, thereby creating a powerful alliance between heaven and earth luck, bringing luck not only to the Southeast but also to the Northwest, directly opposite.

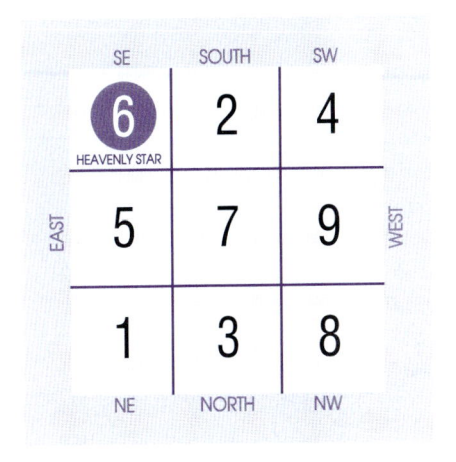

SE	SOUTH	SW
6 HEAVENLY STAR	2	4
5 (EAST)	7	9 (WEST)
1	3	8
NE	NORTH	NW

There is great synergy luck between father and eldest daughter in the family. Should either the master bedroom or the daughter's bedroom be located in the Southeast, unexpected developments take place that

Part 6 : Important Feng Shui Updates for 2011

lift the family fortunes higher than ever. The 6 star brings heaven's celestial blessings and good fortune for those blessed by its cosmic chi. This occurs when your bedroom is located in the Southeast; and if so, do make an effort to fill your room with yang chi energy, a higher noise level and perhaps greater movement in your room. In other words, make it vibrate with energy, as this will energize it, acting as a catalyst for good fortune to occur.

The number 6 signifies authority and power. It is associated with economics and finances. At its peak, 6 stands for authority, influence and control over money. Appearing in the Southeast, it suggests financial management does well under a mature woman.

Within the family, the year suggests that **money should be handled by women**, and power by men. On balance, the male leader has greater strength than the female, but it is the woman who holds the purse strings. This is the way the energies are laid out for the year.

Those observing this pattern of energy and flow with it are most likely to benefit from 2011. It is beneficial to bring this auspicious 6 star to life as it really benefits the entire household, especially in houses where the SE is not a tight corner or a small room that locks up its good energy.

To invoke the best kind of results from the 6 star in 2011, display the **Tree of Wealth** in the SE. Hang **6 large coins** from the tree, and if there are also **6 birds** on the tree, it signifies exciting news coming to the household.

The best way to create this effect is to find a healthy growing tree and place it in the SE before hanging auspicious symbols that ignite the intrinsic power of 6. Remember, 6 birds and 6 large coins will attract heaven luck.

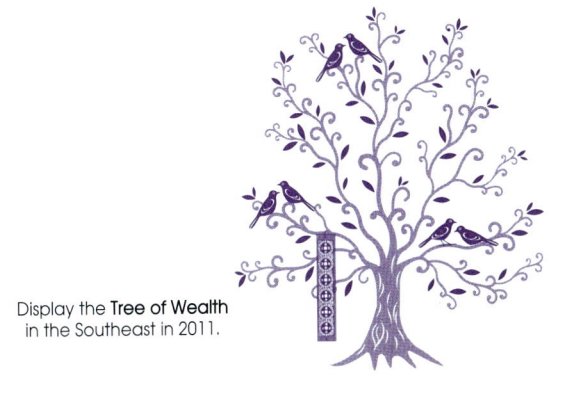

Display the **Tree of Wealth** in the Southeast in 2011.

Magnifying
Victory Luck of 1 in the Northeast

The number 1 star, which brings triumph and success, flies to the Northeast corner in 2011. So anyone who resides in this part of the house benefits from this lucky star number. Anyone living here will feel its benevolent effect, as the number 1 star attracts all kinds of triumphant moments. This kind of luck is especially welcome by those engaged in competitive pursuits, as it helps you win.

In 2011 this star brings winning luck to young men, especially those who are ambitious and keen

SE	SOUTH	SW
6	2	4
5 (EAST)	7	9 (WEST)
1 VICTORY STAR (NE)	3 (NORTH)	8 (NW)

to succeed. What is exciting is that the direction Northeast benefits from three good stars of the 24 mountains, so there is some very exciting potential that can be tapped from this location. It is a good idea to keep the NE energized through the year. Do not let it get too quiet. Yang energy should be created by making sure this part of the house or of your favorite room stays well lit and is occupied. At all costs, prevent *yin spirit formation* by not keeping the sector too silent through the year.

The most auspicious symbols to place here in the NE are all the symbols that signify victory such as awards, certificates, trophies and victory banners. You can also fly a flag in the NE sector this year. The flag always suggests the announcement of victories.

Place the **Victory Banner, one of the 8 Auspicious objects, and a symbol of victory,** in the NE this year.

Benefiting from the Star of Scholarship & Romance in the Southwest

The fourth lucky secondary location of 2011 is Southwest, which benefits from the romance and scholastic star of 4. This is a very powerful star of love and will bring beautiful romantic energy to anyone residing in the Southwest. This is, in any case, the location associated with marriage and domestic happiness. It is also the place of the mother, so the matriarchal force is associated with the SW. With the romantic star 4 placed here, all the stress and strains associated with the five yellow of the past

SE	SOUTH	SW
6	2	**4**
5 (EAST)	7	9 (WEST)
1	3	8
NE	NORTH	NW

year has definitely dissolved. In 2011, this location brings love and marriage opportunities. It also brings better harmony appreciation of the mother families and households.

The number 4 is often associated with romantic peach blossom vibrations, so the luck of this sector directly benefits those still single and unmarried. For those already married, peach blossom brings a happier family life. Domestic energies get enhanced and those who know how to **energize the SW with bright lights** will find the number 4 star will jazz up their love relationships.

The number 4 star is also excellent for those working on getting their diplomas or degrees. It helps scholarship so the Southwest is also beneficial for those sitting for exams this year.

Magnifying the Earth Element to Enhance Resources

Updating feng shui each year involves more than taking care of lucky and unlucky sectors. It also requires being alert to the balance of elements and their effects on the year's energy flows. This is revealed in the year's four pillars chart which, in 2011 indicates an absence of the Earth element in the primary chart of the year.

The intrinsic element of the year as indicated by the heavenly stem of the **Day Pillar** is yang Metal, and altogether there are three Metal elements in the chart. There are also three Wood elements, one Water and one Fire, making then a total of the eight elements that make up the primary chart of the year.

The Earth element is however missing in 2011, and the Earth element symbolizes resources. This makes Earth **a very important element**, because without resources, none of the other indicated attributes such as wealth, success, prosperity, creativity and so forth can manifest.

The Chi Lin with 4 scholastic objects is an excellent activator for the number 4 star in the SW this year.

This is one of the secrets in Paht Chee reading. It is always important that the intrinsic element (in this year, it is Metal) is kept continually replenished by having the element that produces it present. In 2011, this means the Earth element because Earth produces Metal; hence Earth is the resource element for 2011 - do note that this changes from year to year.

As Earth is the missing element this year, anyone who makes the effort to magnify the presence of Earth element in their living spaces is bound to enjoy excellent feng shui. And Earth element is best symbolized by either a **picture of mountains** or better yet, having the presence of crystals, stones and rocks which come from within the earth.

This is the key that unlocks the manifestation of other kinds of luck. It is important to create the presence of Earth element objects in the home and to also strengthen the Earth element corners of the home. These are the SW and NE. Keep these two corners of the home well lit so that the Fire element is ever present to effectively strengthen these Earth element sectors.

The paht chee chart does however show that there is hidden Earth, but here, the Earth element is not immediately available. Nevertheless, it does indicate the availability of hidden resources. When the Earth element gets magnified, the economics of your living situation becomes extremely comfortable.

So do place stones, rocks or crystals - the best are the large circular **crystal globes** - on your coffee table in the living area and then shine a light on it so that the energy of the Earth element gets diffused through the room. Also enhance all compass Earth sectors - NE and SW as well as the center - in the same way. Creating a "*mountain*" with rocks or pebbles in an artistic way also brings excellent feng shui potential. Indeed, it is not only the Chinese who have a tradition of creating "miniature mountains" in and around their gardens and homes. Many other Eastern traditions where feng shui is popularly practiced - such as Japan and Korea - also have their own artistic recreations of mountain scenery. This always signifies the Earth element.

Hidden Earth

We need to look at the entire paht chee chart to highlight the element that is in most short supply; this involves looking at all the elements of the year's chart including the hidden elements.

In 2011, there are three elements of hidden Earth, which bring about a magnification of the Earth element. But in expanding the analysis to include the hidden elements, we need to also take note of the shortage of the Water element. So as in the previous year, the Water element continues to be needed.

In this respect, 2011 is better than 2010, because this year there is one Water element available (last year Water was completely missing). The Hour pillar has Yang Water as its heavenly stem. But Water needs to be supplemented to keep the elements in good balance.

Create a **mountain of pebbles** in your home to activate the all-important resource element of Earth in 2011. The NE and SW activated this way brings valuable hidden resource luck to the home.

Adding to the strength of Water strengthens the Wood element for the year and this is beneficial. This is because Wood symbolizes prosperity and financial success. Hence the placement or addition of the Water element in the Wood sectors East and Southeast creates excellent wealth feng shui.

Under the Eight Aspirations formula, the SE is also the sector that stands for prosperity via the accumulation of wealth. To activate this sector, Water required, but Water without Earth is not as effective as Water with Earth! So what is required is the placement of a **Crystal Water Feature** in the SE corner. This would be then an excellent wealth energizer for 2011. Any kind of water presence for this corner in any room that you frequently use (except your bedroom) would be excellent feng shui.

Nine Wealth Gods to Materialize Prosperity Luck

The final feng shui tip we would like to share with readers for the year is the placement of a ship bringing nine wealth gods sailing into your home. This has great relevance for the year as it suggests that the winds and waters will bring the divine personifications of wealth luck into the home.

Wealth Gods are a very effective for symbolic placement in feng shui folklore, and it is for this reason that the Chinese always invite Wealth Deities into the home. But there are certain years when the Wealth gods are especially effective and that is when the *Big Auspicious* stars of the 24 mountains fly into two opposite primary directions, which is the case in 2011.

Both the North and the South sectors of every home have, and thus can benefit from these stars; but they work only if they can be energized by the presence of Wealth Deities which are believed to bring good cosmic chi into the homes. This will activate the North-South axis. So do place the ship in a North-South orientation within the home.

Place a **crystal water feature** in the Southeast corner of the living room to energize for wealth.

Part 6 : Important Feng Shui Updates for 2011

Powerful Talismans & Amulets For 2011

If you have been following the advice given in these Fortune & Feng Shui books on annual feng shui updates, you are already familiar with the time dimension of feng shui which protects against negative luck each year.

This requires overall cleansing and re-energizing of the energy of the home to prepare for the coming of a new year, while simultaneously making placement changes to accommodate a new pattern of chi distribution. Getting rid of old items and replacing with specially made new remedial cures that are in tune with the year's chi brings pristine and fresh new luck into the home.

The Dog person enjoys the fabulous wealth star of 8 in its feng shui chart this year. Unfortunately the 24 mountains constellation does not predict equally good news, with the *Star of Yearly Conflict* making an appearance to spoil your luck. You may find your temper quicker this year, with an unchracteristic impatience getting the better of you. You are also affected by the *Side Three Killings* which needs to be controlled with suitable cures.

Your Life Force and Inner Essence is weak this year, indicating you are more susceptible to spirit harm and the bad intention of enemies or rivals. But you do enjoy the *Star of Small Auspicious* brought to you from the direction of the Boar. The potential for success is definitely there to be tapped by the Dog person this year, so first you need to ensure the afflictions that affect you are under control; then make the effort to enhance the good stars and to plan your moves according to your good months in order to get the most out of what could be a great year.

Wear Protective Pendants to suppress Three Killings energy

The three killings affliction can cause severe loss that can bring headaches and heartache, and because you are afflicted by it from the side, it is a good idea to stay protected at all times. The best kind of protection against this malicious star is mantra protection. Wear the OM AH HUM pendant to purify all your negative karma arising from negative actions committed through body, speech and mind. When you wear this mantra, you are blessing not just yourself but also purifying the whole enovironment that surrounds you, including the people you encounter in daily life. This mantra will smoothen your path and ensure you are protected from the three kinds of loss brought by the *three killings*.

Dispel Three Killings Chi with the 3 Celestial Protectors

Another powerful cure for the three killings affliction are the three celestial guardians. Depicted with their implements, the Chi Lin carries the Lasso, the Fu Dog carries the Hook, while the Pi Yao has the Sword. Together, these three guardians will dispel the negative energy coming your way from this affliction, protecting against loss of relationships, loss of good name and loss of wealth. Display them in the West part of your living room or home and also in the West of your office. This cure is important for the Dog person because the three killings afflicts you from the side.

Use the Sacred Sunburst to Counter Low Life Force & Inner Essence

The Sacred Sunburst has been designed with rays of light that emanate from a powerful mantra. This cure when placed in your animal sign direction of Northwest will help boost your Life Force and Innver Essence in a year when these elements are weak. When you suffer low life force and inner essence, it is easy to fall victim to spirit harm. It also makes you more vulnerable to black magic and the bad intentions of others who may see you as a rival or nemesis. Stay protected with the Sacred Sunburst displayed in the NW of both your home and your office.

Use the Enhancing Mirror to Absorb the Power of 8 from the NW

The auspicious number 8 star lies in the Northwest this year, the home direction of the Dog. Embrace this good fortune this year with the Enhancing Mirror, which features the **Big Auspicious** word, surrounded by the sacred syllables *Om Ah Hum*; this will absorb power of 8 energy from the Northwest, allowing you to benefit from it. This mirror also works to deflect away bad luck and the evil intentions of others. The more successful you are, the more reason you give others to envy you. Transform negative thoughts from others into positive ones, and turn your rivals into supporters with this sacred mirror.

Suppress Misunderstandings with the Flaming Dharma Wheel

You are afflicted by the Star of Yearly Conflict in 2011, which could make you more quarrelsome than usual. This affliction threatens to affect your relationships both in work and in your personal life. Especially during months when the argumentative Wood star enters your chart, you could find yourself uncharacteristically hot-tempered. Losing your cool could cost you a lot this year. Ensure you don't let this star get the better of you by displaying the Flaming Dharma Wheel in your home. This wheel is the Dhamachakra eight-spoked wheel surrounded by a circle of Fire, which symbolizes Fire and Gold energy. It has the power to reduce gossip, slander and office politics, as well as to help you in the event of any courtcase or legal entanglements you may find yourself embroiled in.

Display the Sacred Mantra Plaque for Protection against Cosmic Negatives

The Four Dharmakaya Relic Plaque protects you from harm and removes all the negative vibes around you, bringing you auspicious luck instead. The Windhorse Plaque protects from harm, fear, contagious disease and fire. Displaying it will also help you keep safe against weapons, fire, water, poison and black magic. It also helps to protect against sickness and contagious diseases. Hang it near your main door.

Enhance your Home Direction with the Water Globe with Tree of Life

This crystal water globe comes with the Tree of Life and the 4 Dharmakhaya mantras at the bottom. Water is the element that appears to be totally missing from the year's Paht Chee chart, so having this water globe will help redress the balance of energies, allowing you to take full advantage of your positive luck this year. The spherical shape of the globe while ensures smooth and harmonious relationships with family, friends, colleagues and within your marriage. Display this water globe in your animal sign location of Northwest, or in the center of your living room.

Make Best Use of Positive Affirmations to Unleash the Power of your Subconscious

Positive words and affirmations when viewed over and over are like mantras that enter your subconscious. This year we have incorporated these affirmative and positive sayings into several of our new items as powerful activators of good luck. Our glass pebbles and mandala stones with positive words and auspicious symbols can be displayed in your animal sign location of Northwest for best effect.

Put them in a pot or bowl in the NW, or even better, load them onto a miniature sailing ship, letting the ship sail in from one of your good directions. You can also add these stones into your mandala offering set.

Sacred Moving Mantra Watches

Moving mantra watches are suitable for any animal sign; anyone can wear them. These watches have been specially designed to bring you the trinity of luck - heaven, earth and mankind luck. There are 3 clocks in this watch, so it can support 3 time zones, but even better, around each dial is a mantra which moves, so every second that passes is like chanting an auspicious mantra. The mantras featured on this watch are the Amitabha Buddha mantra, Manjushri mantra and the Kuan Yin mantra. Wearing this watch will bring protection as well as attract plenty of good fortune and prosperity continuously into your life.

Also available this year are the **Medicine Buddha watch** and the **Green Tara** watch. The **Medicine Buddha watch** has been specially designed to bring good health and longevity, and it comes with the Medicine Buddha mantra and image. The band is embossed with the Medicine Buddha mantra. The mantra is repeated on the face in a moving dial so the mantra is constantly moving. Wearing this watch will bring you protection from sickness. Suitable for those of

Part 7 : Powerful Talismans & Amulets for 2011

you who may be prone to falling sick, or the more elderly among you, to maintain a long, healthy and comfortable life.

The **Green Tara watch** features the beautiful Green Tara in the face. The band of the watch is stamped with Green Tara's mantra - Om Tare Tuttare Ture Soha. This mantra is repeated in a dial on the face which is constantly moving, creating blessings for you all hours of the night and day. Green Tara brings success luck and helps to overcome blocks and obstacles to success. She is also known as the Swift Liberator, known to bring results quickly to those who call on her help.

Table Top Treasures to Enhance Desks and Workspaces

Many of us spend a great deal of our time at our desks and in front of our computers whether during work, play or our spare time. It is always good to energize the immediate space around us with good fortune symbols and items that hold positive meaning for us. We have designed two such items that make simply the most delightful table top treasures, a **miniature photo frame** enameled with peonies, the flower of love, and a **matching clock**. Place photos of your loved ones in such photo frames near you while you work.

This will bring you positive and happy energy, and when you're happy, you become more productive, more peaceful and yes, also more lucky.

Powerful Gemstones to Connect Your Lucky Day with the Seven Most Powerful Planets

The seven planets signify seven days of the week, and connection with each planet is achieved by wearing its correct gemstone. Using your lucky day of the week, you can determine which planet has the luckiest influence on you and which gemstone you should wear or carry close to your body to attract the good luck of that planet. Start wearing the gem on your lucky day and empower with incense and mantras before wearing.

The SUN is the planet of Sunday

This is the principal planet which gives light and warmth, brings fame and recognition and enhances one's personal aura. It is an empowering planet that brings nobility, dignity and power. This gemstone enhances your leadership qualities and increases your levels of confidence so your mind is untroubled and clear. The color that activates the SUN is RED, so all red-colored gemstones are excellent for those of you having SUNDAY as your lucky day based on your Lunar Mansion.

Rubies, **red garnets**, **rubellites** or even **red glass** or **crystal** would be extremely powerful. You can also wear red clothes, carry red handbags to enhance the energy of the Sun, but a red gemstone is the most powerful… Start wearing on a Sunday at sunrise after reciting the mantra here 7 times.

Mantra: *Om Grini Suraya Namah Hum Phat*

The MOON is the planet of Monday

The moon has a powerful influence on your mind, your thoughts and attitudes. Lunar energy is associated with the tides and with water, bringing enormous good fortune to those who successfully activate its positive influences; and is especially suitable for those whose lucky day is Monday.

For energizing lunar energy, the best is to wear the pearl, those created in the deep seas or from the freshwater of rivers. Wearing pearls (any color) bring good habits to the wearer and creates good thoughts. It brings calm, peace of mind, mental stability and good health. It also brings wealth and enhances all positive thoughts. Over time, it engenders the respect of others. Start wearing on a Monday in the evening before sunset and recite the mantra here 11 times.

Mantra: *Om Som Somaya Namah Hum Phat*
The Planet MARS rules Tuesday

This is a masculine planet associated with fiery energy and the power of oratory. Activating Mars brings an authoritative air of leadership and confidence like a general leading troops to war. It brings success and victory in any competitive situation. Worn on a Tuesday, a gemstone that resonates with Mars unleashes all its fiery strength in competitive situations. The most powerful gemstone to activate Mars is **natural red coral**, the deeper the red, the better it will be. Start wearing on a Tuesday one hour after sunrise and after reciting the mantra here 19 times.

Mantra: *Om Ang Anghara Kaya Namah Hum Phat*

The Planet MERCURY rules Wednesdays

To anyone who can successfully activate Mercury, this planet brings great intelligence and amazing analytical capabilities that become vastly enhanced. Mercury increases your ability to learn and your powers of absorption are magnified. The ability to memorize also improves. Mercury facilitates powers of expression and communication. You will work fast and become effective in getting things done. The cosmic color of Mercury is green; **emeralds, green tourmalines, green**

quartz are all suitable. **Green jade** is the most powerful energizer of Mercury. Anyone wearing jade will always be smarter than others and can always outwit anyone. It is a very powerful gemstone. Start wearing on a Wednesday two hours after sunrise and recite the mantra here 9 times.

Mantra: *Om Bhrum Buddhaya Namah Hum Phat*

The Planet Jupiter rules Thursdays

The most auspicious of the seven planets, this planet attracts wealth and brings great influence to those who can successfully activate its powerful energies. To do so requires you to perform many charitable works and then you will need to wear the gemstone of Jupiter that will make you rise to spectacular heights of success. You will become a highly respected leader wielding power and great influence.

Jupiter's energies are transmitted through yellow gemstones the most powerful of which are **yellow sapphires, citrines, topaz** or **flawless yellow-coloured glass** or **crystal**. Wear a yellow sapphire that is flawless and is at least 7 carats big. This brings enormous wealth luck. **Yellow Citrines** or **Imperial Topaz** are also effective. But they must be flawless or you will be quick-tempered and hard to please. Start wearing on a Thursday an hour before sunset after reciting the mantra here 19 times.

Mantra: *Om Bhrim Bhrihas Pataye Namah Hum Phat*

The Planet Venus rules Fridays

This is the planet of love, romance, sexuality, marriage, material comforts, domestic bliss and luxury. Venus brings all kinds of artistic skills to those whose lucky day is Friday and also to those who empower Venus by connecting to it via the wearing of its gemstones. Venus transmits its cosmic energy through flawless diamonds, quartz crystals, zircons, white sapphires, and other colorless gemstones with clear transparency.

Various subtle hues such as pink, yellow and blue tints are suitable for different types of professions and social positions, as long as the gem does not have any solid color. So it is crystalline stones that resonate best with Venus. Start wearing on a Friday at sunrise after you recite the mantra here 16 times.

Mantra: *Om Shum Shukraya Namah Hum Phat*

The Planet Saturn rules Saturdays

This planet governs careers and an empowered or energized Saturn is excellent for overcoming obstacles at the work place. When projects or bosses cause you to stumble or when hindrances stand in the way, it is because Saturn has to be appeased. Those whose lucky day is Friday possess the ability to rise above hardships and obstacles, but enhancing Saturn by wearing its gemstone will empower you even more. Anyone wearing Blue Sapphires can connect directly with Saturn.

Start wearing on a Saturday 2 and a half hours before sunset and recite the mantra here 23 times.

Mantra: *Om Sham Shanay Scaraya Namah Hum Phat*

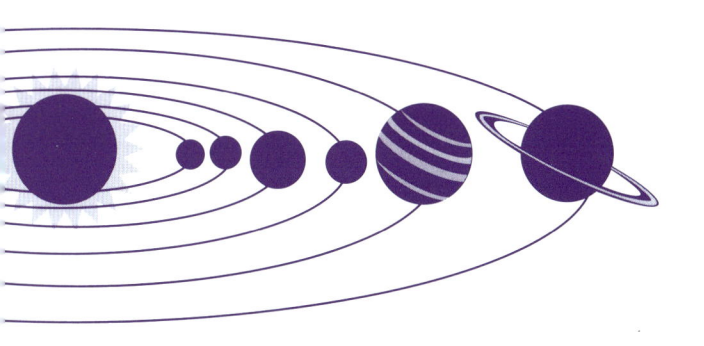

So, What Do You Think?

We hope you enjoyed this book and gained some meaningful insights about your own personal horoscope and animal sign... and you've put some of our feng shui recommendations into practice! Hopefully you are already feeling a difference and enjoying the results of the positive actions you have taken.

But Don't Stop Now!

You can receive the latest weekly news and feng shui updates from Lillian herself absolutely FREE! Learn even more of her secrets and open your mind to the deeper possibilities of feng shui today.

Lillian too's free online weekly ezine is now AVAILABLE

Here's how easy it is to subscribe:
Just go online to www.lilliantoomandalaezine.com and sign up today!